MY NEW PURPOSE

A Retiree's Discovery
in a Children's Hospital ICU

BY DAVID J. DEUTCHMAN

JAKELIRY, LLC

This Children's Hospital is located in a large city somewhere in the United States. In consideration of HIPAA (the Health Insurance Portability and Accountability Act) and out of respect, I chose not to identify the hospital or city in order to provide an extra layer of privacy for the patients and their families. Additionally, all of the names of patients, family members, and hospital staff have been changed.

© Copyright 2018 JAKELIRY, LLC
All rights reserved in whole or in part.

ISBN 978-0-9965828-7-2
Library of Congress Control Number: 2018939083

First Edition
Printed in the United States

Cover and book design by Laurie Goralka Design
Edited by Susan D. Lilly and Bonnie Beach

Cover image: *David with one of "his babies" who was soon to be discharged from the ICU.*

Comments and requests for more information may be emailed to david_923@icloud.com

Acknowledgements

WHEN I STARTED WRITING this book in April of 2016, I realized how very grateful I was for the opportunity to have a meaningful volunteer position with Children's Hospital. Thank you to all at Children's who made that possible and to the staff who have helped make every day there over the last 12 years so memorable.

I'd also like to extend my thanks, admiration, and appreciation to the hundreds of kids and their parents who, through their struggles, have taught me how to give something I never knew I had in me.

My heartfelt thanks to my daughter, Susan Lilly, for her tireless efforts, unlimited patience, and—most importantly—the creative input she summoned to help my thoughts and words come together. I will always fondly remember working on this project with her.

My sincere thanks to my cousin, Adrienne Hickey, who, from the very start of this process, was a tremendous source of information, advice, and genuine encouragement.

Thank you to my daughter, Jill Deutchman, who was also a great resource; I appreciate her guidance and support.

My grandchildren, Eli and Ryan, were a surprising but welcome source of motivation, and I wish to thank them as well.

Finally, thank you to my wife, Ronnie, not only for her understanding and patience when I was holed up, writing for hours—at times during our vacations—but also for the endless encouragement and unwavering support she's provided over the years, especially after some of my toughest days at the hospital. Ronnie, you are my rock, and I love you.

*Dedicated to The Kids
who have touched my heart and enriched my life.*

Table of Contents

	Preface	ix
1	Don't Go Falling in Love	1
2	Now I Know	4
3	Gifts of Kindness	6
4	Why Didn't I Know?	8
5	A Mother's Scream	10
6	The Red Heart	12
7	It Was Deliberate	14
8	Check on Mom	15
9	Don't You Die on Us	17
10	Christmas at Children's	20
11	A Battle Won	22
12	Don't Be Afraid, Baby	26
13	My Little Brothers and Sisters	28
14	Babies I'll Never Forget	33
15	She Was "In There"	35
16	A Heavy Heart	39
17	It's Okay, Buddy	41
18	No Fault of Their Own	43
19	My New Buddy	45

20	"Trauma Houston"	50
21	Pink Sparkle Nail Polish	52
22	"Trachy" Moms	54
23	The Nurses	56
24	My Little Girl	58
25	"Pray for My Son"	60
26	Don't Forget Mom	62
27	Moments	64
28	You're Hired!	69
29	Bring the Baby Back, Stat	73
30	All in One Night	78
31	One Final Wave	82
32	Back to the ICU	85
33	My Babies	87
34	The Xbox Factor	93
35	The Dads	96
36	Final Thoughts	98
	Appendix	104

Preface

The longest and most familiar portion of my adult life was coming to a close and the next stage was unchartered territory.

I began my retirement from Maidenform Worldwide, Inc., in the beginning of 2000 after a 41-year career where, during the last ten years, I was the Senior Vice President for International Sales. For the first few months, I was at a loss as to what to do with my time, and I was motivated to find something meaningful.

I started doing guest lectures on international marketing at four universities, and while I found it both stimulating and rewarding to engage with so many bright young people, there were not enough classes to occupy my time.

Then, as so often happens, a coincidental chain of events came about in 2005 that would change my life.

As an avid runner for more than 25 years, I was dealing with one injury after another. On this particular morning, I had an appointment for a rehab session for my knee (which is still an issue 12 years later), and it was at the building next to Children's Hospital.

I decided to walk into the hospital and see what kind of volunteer opportunities were available. I was directed to the Volunteer Services office where I learned there were a variety of different positions. I had no idea such an incredible journey was about to begin.

The hundreds of children (and their parents) whom I have had the honor of meeting, celebrating with, and—at times—consoling over the last 12 years have compelled me to write this book.

My New Purpose

Their remarkable strength, courage, and resilience, often at times of great loss, have moved me to places that I had never or rarely experienced. In doing so, they taught me more about people and—most especially—about myself.

And so I invite you to join me on this journey, one of the most memorable of my life.

[1]

Don't Go Falling in Love

IT WAS MY FIRST DAY as a volunteer at Children's Hospital, and I was feeling energized and excited.

Though clearly a hospital, it was notably a more cheerful environment than what you might expect. Walls were painted with bright colors, hallways lit up with kid-friendly art and uplifting phrases, and a friendly staff even smiled as they passed me—a stranger to them, at this point.

I met the Director of Volunteer Services, Carolyn Johnson, and she suggested I work in the school program, given my recent experiences guest lecturing. The hospital's school program was designed to help longer-term patients continue their education so they didn't fall behind. Hospital teachers communicated with the child's school to coordinate a continued curriculum.

While I enjoyed interacting with the children, after a few weeks I began to feel that the school program was not the best fit for me. It was during that time, when two events took place in the span of two minutes, that everything changed.

One of my responsibilities for the school program was to escort the children from their rooms to our classroom. Most of the patients had various ports and lines that were connected to a pole, so they needed assistance.

This particular morning, I went to a room on the third floor to pick up a little girl. I met her mother who told me her daughter was scheduled to have surgery in one hour, so she obviously could not attend class. We only spoke briefly then I wished her luck and

My New Purpose

started to leave the room. But she followed me out into the hallway, clearly still wanting to speak with me. She began telling me the details of her daughter's condition—the obstacles she was facing and what was involved in the next surgery.

After several minutes, I again wished her the best and gave her a hug. As I went to pick up another patient, I thought to myself how interesting it was that this woman so needed to speak with someone that she would open up to a virtual stranger.

Then, as I was waiting at the elevator, a young woman approached me from the Pediatric Intensive Care Unit (PICU). She looked pale, exhausted, and worried. As she stood waiting, standing next to me, I quietly asked her if she was okay.

"No," she said, "my son was flown in last night, and he's not doing well at all." She then fell right into my arms and started crying. I embraced her and tried my best to console her.

These two encounters with these two mothers in the span of two minutes made it clear to me what I wanted to do at Children's Hospital.

I went to the volunteer office to request a new assignment, one that would bring me into contact with the parents as well as the kids. I was fortunate that there was an opening in PICU/TICU (Technology-Dependent Intensive Care Unit), and I was transferred there the next week.

My new assignment was to work for a Child Life specialist named Shirley who had many years of experience in PICU and TICU. Child Life specialists are pediatric health care professionals who help the children and their families cope with the many challenges of hospitalization, illness, and disability. They provide important support for the family and siblings during what can often be a very difficult time.

And so began my orientation to the various units where I would be working.

There are "Patient Care Areas" that are internally referred to as "PCAs" or "the floor." The children on these floors are sick enough to be admitted but will generally be discharged in two to five days, so it was considered a high-turnover unit.

The Technology-Dependent Intensive Care Unit was for patients who were more seriously sick or injured, but here, too, many would ultimately be discharged with a positive outcome. Many, but not all.

I would be spending most of my time initially with the TICU and PICU.

For much of that first day, Shirley gave me a broad overview of what I would be doing. Basically, I was to help provide whatever needs of the day that the patients or their families had. I learned this primarily involved "supportive care"; in other words, holding babies, visiting and reading, even singing to the children. And then, for the parents, I would be a listener, a shoulder to cry on, and a safe person for them to talk to and be with.

What remained unspoken was that I would be seeing some very tough situations. Certainly, Shirley would be watching my reactions to see if I could handle being in these units.

The first patient I met on that initial day was a ten-year-old girl named Cindy who, developmentally, was more like a five-year-old. Apparently, she never smiled at anyone but, for whatever reason, she smiled at me when I walked through the door, and I was quickly taken by her.

When I arrived for my next shift the following week, I asked Shirley how Cindy was doing. She said she'd gone to "the floor," and then she very specifically added, "Let me tell you something, David. Don't go falling in love with these kids." And I didn't, until I did, and it took its toll.

[2]

Now I Know

IT DIDN'T TAKE LONG to learn about loss and loneliness in the Intensive Care Units (ICUs). I was walking through PICU when I saw a little girl in one of the rooms who appeared to be peacefully sleeping. A nurse told me she was flown in overnight from a town 100 miles away following a serious car accident. Her mother died on the scene, and although this child technically died shortly after arriving at the hospital, she was on life support to keep her organs ready for donation.

I learned there were seven children who would benefit from this generous and selfless act of love. I looked deeply at that beautiful girl and thought about how her heart would continue to live in another child's body, perhaps beating for another 50 years or more. The cycle of her life and death and then, amazingly, another child's life would be able to continue.

The last child I saw that day was a five-year-old girl named Latisha who was brought in under the custody of the Department of Family and Children's Services (DFACS). Many of these DFACS children were abused or neglected while others had parents who were addicts, absentee, or incarcerated. These kids typically wouldn't have any family visiting them, so I made it a priority to spend more time with her.

I found Latisha alone in her room with a thin board taped to her wrist to hold the various lines running into her. I introduced myself and asked her if she would like me to read a book to her. She quickly said, very softly, "Yes, please."

The moment I opened the book, she reached up with her right hand, the one with the lines hooked up to it, and took my hand. She held my hand for the entire time I read to her and then fell asleep after a while. I was so touched by her, knowing that it must have been difficult to hold her arm like that, but that was how badly she wanted to hold my hand.

When I left the room I looked back at her, that sweet, small child so very alone, and for the first time of what would be many, I had to fight back tears. I thought to myself, "Now I know what I want to do with the rest of my life."

It was only the following week when another DFACS child would steal my heart. I was in the PICU reviewing the "census" with Shirley. The census is a complete list of every patient in the ICUs. Shirley would go down the list and brief me on which patients I should focus on and if there was a particular parent who could use more support.

The first thing Shirley asked me to do that morning was to spend some time with a child who had been severely abused and was now under DFACS custody. She told me the room number but, after checking my list, I was confused, because it showed the patient listed as a four-week-old baby. But Shirley confirmed that, in fact, it was the right room and the right patient. I must have looked shocked, as I found it inconceivable that anyone could abuse a newborn baby.

In any event, I held her closely for nearly two hours. I whispered healing thoughts as I once again was drawn to a DFACS child. They had no one in the world to care for them, to worry about them, love them or cry for them. So I would do that.

[3]

Gifts of Kindness

SOME OF THE MOST DIFFICULT cases I saw were the abused babies and children brought into the ICUs. We saw a lot of babies with "shaken baby syndrome," which had terrible and irreversible consequences. Babies can die from this syndrome, and many who survive often suffer lifelong symptoms such as vision loss, learning disabilities, and/or brain damage.

In some cases, small babies were classified as a "non-accidental trauma" or "NAT." While a toddler could have traumatic injuries from running or falling, a baby who could not yet walk or run, let alone get out of his infant seat, was not capable of an accidental injury.

These NAT babies were therefore suspected to be victims of abuse. In these cases, radiological images often showed evidence of prior traumatic injuries, confirming that the infant had been abused for all of his young life. Each child abuse case triggered a chain of protocoled reactions. Doctors, nurses, social workers, case management representatives, DFACS, and law enforcement were all involved on behalf of the child.

I came to develop great respect for the people who worked for DFACS to help these children. The hundreds of things they did right often went unnoticed, but the moment one thing went wrong, it tarnished what was otherwise a job done well.

I also came to have new respect for foster parents who took home many of our abused children when they were discharged. Several others I got to know would foster special needs children, which was an amazing gift of kindness. Even though there were a few foster parents I had issues with, there were countless others that I genuinely admired and respected.

[4]

Why Didn't I Know?

THEN 18-MONTH-OLD NICKY broke our hearts. He had been vomiting for a couple of days, saw his pediatrician, and was sent home with the reasonable expectation that he would soon get better. After all, "there was a lot of that going around," and according to his parents, there seemed to be nothing remarkable about Nicky's condition.

When another two days went by with no improvement, his parents took their son back to their physician, and this time, Nicky was admitted to Children's for a more detailed assessment.

Within a couple of days, Nicky's parents received the diagnosis of glioblastoma, an extremely serious brain tumor. From that point on, the news kept getting worse, day after day. First, they learned his tumor was inoperable. A day later, they were told chemotherapy was not an option, and then they were informed that radiation treatment would not help him. Nicky's parents were quickly realizing the severity of their son's condition.

Whenever I would meet a new family like this, I would try to "read the room" before I entered. I could usually tell from body language if the parents wanted privacy or were open to me coming in to check on them.

In this case, Nicky's father, Michael, was the one I began to visit, talk with, and see how I could help. But I never did engage with Nicky's mom because my sense was that she wanted her privacy and wasn't looking for conversation.

Nicky was not expected to survive more than another couple of weeks. He was intubated, sedated, and in no obvious distress. Michael had put a picture of him on a desk next to his crib. It was one of those classic one-year-old photos where the baby is smiling, all dressed up, looking as happy and healthy as could be.

During one visit with Michael by my side, I looked down at Nicky while holding his little helpless hand. At that moment, Michael said to me, "That's not my son," and, pointing to the picture on the desk, he said, "That's my son over there."

Nicky died a day later and everyone in the unit took it very hard, especially me. I had developed a relationship with Michael, and to see him grieving for the sudden loss of his son was devastating.

When I write about this now, some six to eight years later, I admonish myself for not having tried harder to talk with Nicky's mom, to put my arms around her and embrace her. Working in the ICUs, there was a fine line between being supportive and becoming intrusive.

But in this case I felt I let this mom down. How could I have been so careless? Didn't I know her heart was breaking?

[5]

A Mother's Scream

I WILL NEVER FORGET the first time I heard a mother scream. It was when I was in the TICU. While many patients started in the NICU, if they still required intensive care after a few months, they were transferred to TICU.

Several patients had breathing tubes and were on ventilators. They require suctioning at least every hour and are closely monitored 24/7.

One morning in TICU, Shirley was giving me a new assignment. Mid-sentence, there was a sudden, horrific scream coming from a patient room nearby. It was piercingly intense and accompanied by sobs of "no, no!" It stopped me in my tracks.

I looked over toward that room. The curtain was closed, but the cries permeated through. After a few seconds, I realized that Shirley was watching me. I said to her, "Sorry, I was distracted for a moment. Where were we?"

I was beginning to learn that these things happen, often without warning. In each case, they require a calm reaction from the entire staff. For the parents in the other rooms, however, it can be quite unnerving. They might wonder if one day that scream would be coming from them.

A few days later, I was visiting a one-year-old in TICU with multiple issues. There was a young physical therapist, Emily, working with her. As she was holding the baby's hands she said, "Oh, Katie, Katie, with all your problems, how do you manage to still look so cute?"

Emily asked me how I was dealing with all of "this." I explained to her that, somehow, the moment I walked into the hospital, I was able to disconnect from the emotional connection.

She said she wished she could do that. I asked her if it was getting to her, and she nodded "yes" and began to cry. I offered her a hug and she came into my arms, sobbing.

After I left the room, one of the nurses asked me about what had happened. I was surprised when I had trouble answering her. I found that most of the time, we were able to handle even the most challenging of situations. But when one of us lost our composure, it impacted all of us.

[6]

The Red Heart

MOST VOLUNTEERS WORKED three-hour shifts, but I usually worked six hours. I found that my time there moved very fast and there was always something challenging to do.

Every once in a while we would get a case where a freak accident had devastating consequences. Tammy was a four-year-old girl who came in with multiple, traumatic injuries from a car wreck and was paralyzed from the waist down. I would read to her, play with her, and act silly to make her laugh. She was adorable, and we quickly became buddies.

Tammy would be discharged for a couple of weeks then readmitted for one thing or another. During one of our visits, I drew a picture with a large smiley face. On the bottom, I put a red heart and wrote "David" with an arrow through the heart and "Tammy" underneath it. She loved it, and when she was discharged a month later, she made sure her mom brought that picture home.

Sadly, Tammy soon returned with respiratory issues that had occurred before but now were much more severe. I visited with her many times over several weeks.

One day, when I first arrived in PICU, Shirley spotted me and quickly approached. She wanted to let me know that Tammy had died about 20 minutes prior and that her mother was still in the room.

I stood in the hallway and heard Tammy's mother's cries. When I looked up, all I could see was that drawing I made for Tammy hanging over her bed.

My New Purpose

David with one of "his babies" who was soon to be discharged from the ICU.

[7]

It Was Deliberate

I HAD BEEN IN THE PICU for several months when there was another sudden, tragic event. Two families with young children were leaving a fast food restaurant when a man drove his car into the group, backed up, and then drove into them again. Two of the three kids brought into the hospital were about four years old and suffered broken bones but were stable. However, the other child, Ellie, a two-year-old little girl, suffered a severe TBI (traumatic brain injury), and it soon became apparent that she would not survive.

Family and friends who came to see her all left in tears. Kids get sick and kids get injured, but this deliberate act of violence made it harder to deal with.

When I saw Ellie's grandma in the waiting room, she was sobbing on the phone. After she hung up, I went to try and comfort her. I held her hand and wrapped my arm around her. I did not say anything; there was nothing that could be said.

Soon after, I was asked to join the family. One of the girl's uncles was a preacher and he led about six of us in a beautiful prayer. What moments before was a sterile waiting room was now filled with emotion as we stood holding hands, mourning.

Ellie died later that day.

[8]

Check on Mom

DURING MY FIRST YEAR at the hospital, there was a simple personnel change that would have an unexpected impact on my volunteer career.

Shirley, my supervisor from Child Life, left the hospital. Things like this happened often in my business life, so I wasn't surprised. I was grateful that Shirley had brought me into the PICU, and I have fond memories of her.

A young woman named Lori took over Shirley's position, and during her first few weeks on the job, she spoke with the ICU nurses, social workers, doctors, and the chaplain to best understand their needs.

After about a month, we met. She told me she understood from staff input that I had a unique skill set, and she wanted to change my priorities in the ICUs. She asked me to focus all of my time on the kids and the parents. That change would bring even more challenges and more sadness than I could have foreseen.

Soon I was volunteering three days a week, which was unusual for volunteers at Children's. But I found my revised responsibilities rewarding and enjoyed being in this stimulating atmosphere. I wanted to be there.

Each morning Lori went over my priorities for that day, which always included a visit to the new admits to "check on Mom." Lori also filled me in on any problems, sensitive issues, very sick patients, or any child who was left alone a lot.

My New Purpose

By the time I would see them, the mothers of new admits had typically been up all night. Usually they hadn't eaten since they arrived, and I tried to coax them into going to the cafeteria, offering to stay with their child until they returned. Only a few of the moms took me up on it.

In one case, one of the mothers asked me if this was a standard service of the hospital. I explained to her that while priority-one was to take care of the sick and injured children, we wanted to make sure we took care of our moms, too.

[9]

Don't You Die on Us

I WAS ABOUT TO FACE what would clearly be one of my worst days ever. Everyone who worked in the PICU understood we would occasionally lose a child, but having two children die on the same day was extremely rare.

There was a little girl about five years old named Grace who was admitted with seizures. Over a period of two weeks, her condition steadily worsened and she had to be intubated. She had a lot of other medical issues in addition to the seizures that I didn't know about.

I had visited with her mother, Nicole, but as Grace's condition rapidly declined, my time with her was limited. Grace's grandmother and I had also had occasion to talk, and she confirmed my worst fear: Grace was not going to get better.

When I came in the following week, Grace was in what was termed "end-stage," and the family had made a decision to remove her life support. This process was referred to as "de-escalation." I saw a lot of friends and family in the waiting room, clearly distraught, trying to comfort each other. I saw Nicole briefly and gave her a hug that lasted a few moments longer than usual. It was a heartbreaking scene.

Then I learned that another little girl roughly the same age, Angela, had been transferred from another hospital just days earlier. I didn't know anything about her condition but was quickly informed that she, too, was critically ill and not expected to live through the day. A decision was made to transfer a couple of patients elsewhere in the ICU to allow these two children and their families more privacy in a smaller section of the unit.

By late morning they had de-escalated Grace, now lying on her bed in her room lit only by natural light coming in through the window. Nicole had written a letter to her little girl and was sitting there alone, reading it to her.

I happened to walk past the door, not realizing that Nicole was there, when I heard what she was reading. Slowly, quietly, and surprisingly calm, she read the most poignant and loving words you could imagine. I turned away to give Nicole the privacy she deserved and to also contain the tears I felt welling up in my eyes. And as I started to leave, I heard that loud, piercing, heartbreaking scream I had already heard too many times.

I looked into Angela's room and saw her mother on her knees on the floor, grasping the bars on the side of her baby's bed, hopelessly screaming. Angela's father was on the floor, hugging his wife, their profound anguish and pain running through my body like a current of electricity.

I decided to go down to the NICU and hold a baby, knowing that would have a calming effect on me. I went up to the NICU charge nurse and told her, "Hey, I need a baby to hold." The nurses in NICU had already heard about what had happened in PICU, so they understood.

I was directed to Isabella, who had come in a few days before with a syndrome that resulted in cranial-facial disorders. The sides of her mouth were pointed downwards, giving the baby a seemingly very sad appearance. I held Isabella, this very special child, and softly sang to her.

The nurse told me that although her mother, Marianna, visited every day, she hadn't yet held her baby. Instead, she would sit by the crib, weeping.

At some point while I was holding Isabella, her mother came in, sat down in a chair next to me, and immediately started to cry. She was Latino and spoke very little English, but we still managed to communicate to a degree.

My New Purpose

When our conversation came to a pause, I looked at Marianna, gently placed my hand on her cheek, and said, "Momma, your baby needs you to hold her."

Through tears, Marianna nodded. Then she whispered, "Yes."

As she stood, I motioned to a nurse to help me transfer the baby to her mother. Marianna gave a smile, one that I thought was communicating, real or imagined, "Thank you for helping me do this."

I went back to the PICU and found a nine-year-old girl named Emma who had come up from the oncology unit to recover from surgery. Her head was shaved and had large staple stitching from one side to the other.

I asked her if she wanted anything, and we decided on stickers. She looked up at me with a smile that could light up a room. She was a disarming child.

On my way to the supply closet, I passed through the area where we lost those two darling angels earlier. The unit was now dark and quiet, the tragedies of the day over, the parents now at home making funeral arrangements, buried in their grief.

I found the stickers and some paper for Emma. She looked up as I handed everything to her, once again giving me that endearing smile, thanking me. She was so grateful for so little. I knew her for five minutes and already adored her.

Please, sweet girl, you darling child, don't you die on us.

[10]

Christmas at Children's

CHRISTMAS WAS ALWAYS a very special time, even in the hospital. Hallways were decorated, and it was an appropriately festive environment. In early December, carolers from a local church visited and went around singing to the children and their parents.

On Christmas Day, I escorted Santa Claus around the floors. It was wonderful to see the reaction of the children. Many of them were able to walk out into the hall, and the ones who stayed in bed got a special visit from Santa as well. Sometimes there were extremely critical patients, and I had to keep Santa out of those rooms entirely. It was the nature of the ICUs.

There were "pay it forward" traditions in the units. Mothers who had previously had a child in PICU catered a lunch on Christmas Day for all the moms who were there with their children. In NICU, the alumni moms donated gifts for the babies who were there. The gift bags on every crib lit up the NICU and certainly gave the parents some joy during the holidays.

During the week before Christmas, the doctors tried hard to discharge as many patients as they could, but when I arrived at the hospital every day, the first thing I checked was how many new admits we had from the night before. I hurried to those rooms right away to see the families.

On one particular day, we had a severe trauma case come in the night before. A three-year-old boy named Bobby was involved in a tragic accident when he fell out of a two-story window, which was left open because of a smoky cooking odor. Bobby suffered severe traumatic injuries, including a fractured back and a TBI.

I met his parents, Jim and Jennifer, early that morning, and we quickly developed a warm relationship. When Jim saw a large duffel bag of toys that was left by the room on Christmas morning, he asked me how much he owed for the toys. I felt like hugging him, but it seemed awkward, so I didn't. What I didn't know then was that Bobby would be in the hospital many months and I would spend a lot of time with Jennifer and Jim, often sharing an embrace or a tear.

Some men have a thing about hugging another man, but there were times when I felt it was the right thing to do. In those instances, I didn't hesitate.

During the months that Bobby was with us, I continued to talk a lot with Jennifer, learning about their family and just keeping them company. It was not unusual for me to visit her three times a week, sometimes talking for an hour in Bobby's room. Needless to say, she was totally shattered and I tried hard to convince her to stop blaming herself. So many terrible accidents can happen so quickly, and Jen only planned to keep that window open for a few minutes.

Bobby made some progress in rehab, but he ended up leaving the hospital with multiple disabilities.

I always found it very hard to say goodbye to the parents after sharing their ordeal for such a long time. And so often, their child was being discharged in a diminished state. This was a tough one.

I hugged Jim and then put my arms around Jennifer as we stood hugging each other, both of us trying to find the right moment to let go.

[11]

A Battle Won

THE FIRST BABY I ever held in the Neonatal Intensive Care Unit was a three-month-old baby boy named Bryan. Within two minutes of holding him, he was peacefully asleep, and he became my new best friend. Bryan was one of many reasons the nurses would come to call me the "Baby Whisperer."

The NICU was quite different from the other units at Children's. It was quieter and kept dark, and at a pretty cool temperature because of all of the machines. What made it unique was that it was the only surgical NICU in a wide region.

There were various types of problems seen in the NICU at Children's, some more common than others. There were, of course, a lot of premature babies, those born as much as three to four months early and some weighing as little as two pounds. Many faced a long period of highly specialized care.

Ten years ago, many "preemies," after spending several months in the NICU, ended up with developmental disabilities. But in recent years, more preemies were discharged sooner and with much better outcomes.

I began spending one of my volunteer days each week in the NICU visiting multiple babies each day, and I came to love it. It was hard to remember the names of all of them, but then there were the ones I would never forget. Trey was one of them.

Trey was born prematurely and suffered from multiple medical problems, including some that presented feeding and respiratory issues.

My New Purpose

I visited Trey's mother, Annie, every time I came to the hospital. Usually there were more mothers than fathers visiting their children, but in this case, Trey's father, Chuck, was often at the hospital.

Annie had placed a picture of Trey's three-year-old sister in his crib. When there was a pause in the conversation I was having with Annie, I said to her, "Tell me about your little girl." Annie smiled broadly and joyfully told me all about her. She described her as an adorable, bright little girl who was preschool age, and I continued to ask a few other questions.

Sometimes parents needed a little distraction from the 24/7 of worry.

I was holding Trey one day, and everything was calm until he started regurgitating mucus and turning blue. It hadn't reached the point to trigger one of the medical alarms, but I quickly alerted his nurse anyway.

She yelled out, "Respiratory, Bed 9," and within a few seconds, help of all kinds came to him. There were six or seven people around his crib, and they quickly got everything under control. While they were tending to him, the unit secretary announced, "Mom for Bed 9 coming back."

One of the nurses asked me to intercept Trey's mom to see if I could stall her from returning to the room so that she would be shielded from all of the commotion. I found her and told her that the doctors were in the middle of a small procedure and suggested we hang for a minute. That worked for about 20 seconds, but I could tell by the frantic look on her face that she wasn't buying it. So I took her back to her son. There was still quite a bit of activity with the nurses assisting his breathing, but Trey's color had improved and he appeared to be stabilized.

It was a tough road for Trey. The respiratory issues had become bad enough that the doctors ultimately decided, with the parents' approval, to do a tracheostomy, a procedure that would create a surgical airway in the windpipe. The "trach," as it was referred to, helped with Trey's breathing, but it also required more monitoring and frequent suctioning, all very familiar to the NICU staff.

The procedure went well and Trey was no longer in respiratory distress. For the first time since he was admitted, things began to look positive. I remember Chuck said to me that afternoon, "This is the happiest day of my life."

Then, just a day later, things changed for the worse, and the worry and despair were suddenly etched on their faces once again. I chose not to say anything when I left them that day but, as I passed Chuck's chair, I put my hand on his shoulder and gently squeezed it. Then I walked out the door.

It was Christmastime, and Annie brought their daughter, Cassie, in to visit Trey, who was now in the TICU and improving every day.

The hospital made it a point to have gifts available for siblings of patients who would visit. I took a large toy house with a kitchen set and put it in Trey's room with Cassie's name written on it in big letters. She and her parents were thrilled when they saw it, and I was glad to help make their Christmas Day a little bit merrier.

The time ultimately came when Trey was going to be discharged, and I was so happy I was there that day to say goodbye. Annie put her arms around me and gave me a big hug. Then, two seconds later, she gave me another hug, started to cry, and said, "Oh, David, you were there with us from Day One."

Chuck arrived a few minutes later and, as we were saying our goodbyes, he hugged me as well, and I heard Annie ask him if he was crying. I could tell it was going to be my turn next, and so after our final goodbye, I left the room, choking back my own emotions. I really loved this family.

About six months later, I saw them all while they were in the hospital for one of Trey's check-ups. They reported that he was healthy and everything was going very well.

Trey and his family were in attendance at one of our recent annual NICU reunions hosted for all of our "graduates." I practically jumped out of my chair when I saw them walk in. Trey was sporting a cool, new haircut and looked great. He was clearly continuing to enjoy good health.

When we were all saying goodbyes this time, Chuck and I shook hands, both of us smiling, and we lingered for an extra few moments, just looking at each other. Words were not necessary.

[12]

Don't Be Afraid, Baby

IT DIDN'T TAKE LONG before I learned about the very sick babies that had DNR orders, or "Do Not Resuscitate." The first time I actually held a DNR baby, one of the nurses came up to me to make sure I knew and realized that if he stopped breathing, staff wouldn't come running in to resuscitate him. I told her I completely understood. Over the years, I would hold perhaps 15 to 20 babies with DNR orders.

Jeremy was one of those babies who I held several times over many months. Not only born premature, his medical problems were so dire that he had DNR orders, as agreed upon with his parents.

One day, a NICU nurse told me Jeremy was declining rapidly and would not likely live through the day. In cases like these, the nurses would try to alternate holding a baby for 20 minutes so that he wouldn't be alone. On this particular day, they had several high-acuity babies and were expecting two new admits that morning. Because of that, Jeremy's nurse asked me if I would be willing to hold him and, of course, I agreed without hesitation.

When I first saw Jeremy that day, I could see that the little guy was in a terrible state and in obvious distress. He was lying on his stomach, shaking and gasping, and his body would go into a shuddering spasm as he finally sucked in one more breath. Then the process would begin all over again. It was a heartbreaking scene: This poor baby was suffering.

His oxygen saturation levels, or "sats," were in the 80s instead of the 90 to 100 range, which was considered normal. But that was only the beginning.

My New Purpose

I picked Jeremy up and cuddled him in my arms as I sat down. He immediately stopped shaking and gasping for air, and although his breathing was shallow, he became much more at ease. It was the start of our three-hour journey together.

His sats dropped steadily, into the 70s, 60s, and then—going into the third hour—the 50s. I began talking to him very softly, saying, "Don't be afraid, baby, I've got you."

Once Jeremy's sats passed through the 40s, a few nurses gathered around, and his doctor came over as well. As his sat level dropped to 33, the doc said, "This is it. It's happening now."

I said again, "Don't be scared, baby, I'm here," and I kissed his forehead.

Jeremy quietly stopped breathing and died in my arms.

[13]

My Little Brothers and Sisters

WHEN I STARTED WRITING this book, I never intended to write about my childhood, but I realized there was a relevant connection.

I was asked to visit a 12-year-old child named Julia who, developmentally, was more like six years old. She was a sweet child who only wanted me to hold her hand. After I had been with her for 20 minutes she fell asleep, and I was still holding her hand when a young woman walked in from an organization called "ChildKind."

When DFACS children were discharged, they were often placed in foster care, and ChildKind helped with the transition, especially when there were children with complex care needs or developmental disabilities.

This bright young woman, Caroline, was very interested in my background, how I came to Children's, and what I liked most about volunteering. At some point, she asked me if I would be willing to volunteer an additional day a week for her organization. While I was flattered, I told her that I didn't think I could commit to another day. But there was much more to it that I was reluctant to share.

One might wonder, with all that I had already seen at the hospital, why it would be so difficult for me to help transition these children from DFACS to foster care. I had come into contact with dozens of DFACS kids during my initial years at Children's and had become emotionally connected to many of them. But I realized that there were some things about my personal background that may shed more light on why I was reluctant to participate in the ChildKind program.

My New Purpose

I was born in New York City in the height of the Great Depression, the youngest of three boys. When I was a year old, we moved from the Bronx to Scranton, Pennsylvania, for my father to pursue a business opportunity.

The night we arrived in Scranton, my dad took us to a cafeteria for dinner, all the while knowing he didn't have any money to pay. As it turned out, the owner of the cafeteria was very understanding and, ultimately, he and my dad became good friends.

My oldest brother, who was nine when we moved, would be my source of that story and many more. He told me years later that we lived in the poorest neighborhood imaginable, and that my dad had to walk several miles to get to work because he couldn't spare an extra nickel to take the bus.

We scraped along for the next seven years in a state between poverty and barely getting by. By mid-1942, however, things began to improve when my father's business received a contract from the government to manufacture uniforms for the Women's Army Corps. Unfortunately, this good fortune was short-lived.

My father died on New Year's Eve of 1942. I was eight years old, and it was a loss I would mourn for my entire life.

So there we were, my mother and her three boys, at this time living in a couple of rooms underneath a small grocery store in an alley where the garbage pails were kept. My mother had three siblings and aging parents, all living in New York City. Understandably, she was drawn to her family and so, one month after our father died, we moved back to the Bronx. My brothers and I were suddenly taken out of our school and away from our friends. We left our "apartment" on a bitter cold, snowy night to board a train in Scranton headed to New York. The train was delayed for over an hour because of the snow, and I clearly remember sitting there, staring out the window for that entire time, quietly crying but not wanting my mother to see me.

When the train left and started to pick up speed, I had a rush of thoughts, although I couldn't possibly have articulated them. But I remember the emotions with complete clarity. If I could have put words to them, they would have been, "We're on our way now, headed to a new life. It will be a life of uncertainty, insecurity, and diminished expectations."

We moved into a small, third floor walk-up apartment in the Bronx. I didn't have any friends, and my oldest brother joined the Navy and left for San Diego.

My most vivid memory of the next five years was that of my mother crying and going for long walks at night. My life was filled with sadness, loneliness, and depression. I was lost.

This all changed when I was 12 years old. My grandmother died, and we moved into her two-bedroom apartment a few blocks away. We had to rent out one of the bedrooms to a boarder to help pay the rent. I shared the other bedroom with my middle brother, and my oldest brother (who had returned from the Navy) slept in a den that also served as my mother's bedroom and our dining room.

I soon made a lot of friends and found myself playing stickball 12 hours a day. My life had finally improved. Still, the unhappiness and sadness of the previous five years wouldn't leave me, even when I was living in happier times.

So why have I told you this story? What has driven me to write about a part of my life that I never thought I would ever reveal to anyone? Let us return to the children in DFACS custody.

We know most of these kids were neglected, ignored, or abused. I identified with their fear, loneliness, and helplessness about their future. That was why I was so drawn to them at Children's Hospital.

My New Purpose

I worried about them: Would they be treated well, fed, and loved? And who would wipe away their tears and comfort them when they were afraid? They were my little brothers and sisters.

So now, knowing more about my background, imagine how difficult it would be for me to transition a child from DFACS to the unpredictable life in a new foster home. How could I take the hand of a tearful little boy, walk him into a strange place, his little body shaking in fear, and leave him? Leave him to a life of uncertainty where all that was certain was a life filled with anxiety and doubt.

We are all the sum of the history of our lives, and I just couldn't do that.

David (in his mother's lap) and his family, circa 1939.

[14]

Babies I'll Never Forget

EVERY ONCE IN A WHILE, I found myself connecting new experiences at Children's with ones from my working days. Spending time in the NICU made me think about a memorable moment when I was on a business trip to the Far East.

I was in Hong Kong completing a three-week trip in Asia. We had finished earlier than expected and Liz, our Asian sales manager, suggested we take a trip to Shenzhen, a small but rapidly growing city in Guangdong Province, about a 90-minute train ride from Hong Kong.

Like Manila, Bangkok, and many other Asian cities—with the notable exception of Singapore—we saw many children begging on the streets. It was not unusual or surprising, but when we got to the train station to leave, I saw a truly horrific sight.

There were four small newborn girls lying naked on the ground, only two to four weeks old. Two of them were clearly dead and the other two barely alive. China had a "one-child" law designed to control population growth, and the Chinese placed a much greater value on male babies.

There was a bowl in front of each baby to place money. Staged in front was a girl about ten years old who had had both of her arms crudely amputated to enhance her potential to beg. She had a bucket tied around her neck, and she tried to keep moving in front of me in an effort to ensure my donation. But I felt that giving her money would justify the horror of the whole thing, and I managed to get around her.

At this point, Liz was yelling at me to hurry up and leave the area. She was afraid I might pull out my camera and take pictures of the babies. Liz later explained that, had I done so, I probably would have been arrested, gone to jail, and may not have been heard from for weeks.

Even without photographs, the images of those babies would never leave me.

[15]

She Was "In There"

EVERY TIME I ARRIVED at Children's Hospital, I wondered about what the day would hold, the children I would meet, what their needs would be, and how I could help. On this particular day, I met a family who I would eventually join for a difficult and very sad journey.

I had my morning meeting with Lori to discuss the new admits and outline my priorities for that day, which included the request that, to this day, still gives me chills: "Check on Mom."

This particular day, "Mom" was a woman named Sarah, and when I went to check on her, she appeared very calm and composed. I also met her husband, Justin, later that day.

Their 17-year-old daughter, Catherine, was in the hospital with severe respiratory complications from lissencephaly, a condition she was born with. Lissencephaly was a rare brain malformation that happened in the second trimester of pregnancy. The prognosis largely depended on the severity of the malformation, but many children with this illness had seizures, significant developmental delays, and severe respiratory problems. Their life expectancy was typically about ten years.

Then there were patients like Catherine who, at 17, had beaten those odds. Sadly, she was now at the end-stage of her long battle.

I became very close with Sarah and Justin, having had many long talks and meeting several members of their church, who provided never-ending love and support to them.

My New Purpose

One day they came to me with a special request. Their older daughter, Erin, was in the Army training to become a medic, and she was about to graduate from a base in Oklahoma.

As you can imagine, when a family had a special needs child, life was never the same for any of them. So here was Erin about to graduate and her sister, Catherine, was in the final days of her life. Their parents were faced with a very difficult decision: Should they stay by Catherine's bedside or go to their other daughter's graduation?

They decided that, after not being able to be there for so many things in Erin's life, this time they would go. Sarah and Justin told me of their plans and that they would be away from the hospital for two and a half days. While they had some people from their church who volunteered to stay with Catherine, there was one day still not covered. They asked me if I would take that day and, without hesitation, I accepted.

A few days before they left, I was in Catherine's room when her mother came in. Sarah greeted her daughter, leaned very close to her, and explained that they were leaving for a couple of days, but that she wouldn't be left alone. I saw Catherine nodding her head, as if saying "yes," she understood.

Typically, children with lissencephaly have limited brain function and no ability to communicate. I shared what I had witnessed with one of my supervisors and explained that Catherine apparently understood what her mother was saying. But she expressed serious doubt, believing that Catherine likely couldn't understand anything. I know that's what "the book" says, but I left that day believing there might be more to it in this case.

The day came when I was staying with Catherine at the hospital. When I first arrived, I saw a "Remembrance Book" that her father had left with a note requesting that all of us connected with Catherine's care write a few words. I made a mental note to do that before I left.

But first I greeted Catherine and softly spoke to her. I explained that I was going to keep her company that day and reminded her that her parents went to Erin's graduation. Then I paused and said, "Okay?" As she had done with Sarah, Catherine again nodded as if she understood.

Later in the morning, I told her I had to leave the room for a few minutes and would be back very soon, and I said, "Okay?" And again, she nodded.

I was curious if the tone of saying "okay" was triggering her to nod her head, so I decided to ask her something in a different way. I took her hand and put my other hand on her shoulder. I looked very deeply into her eyes and saw her staring at me in the same way. I said to her, very softly and without the tone of an obvious question, "Catherine, you understand every word I'm saying to you, don't you."

She nodded "yes," and at that moment, I felt that she not only understood me, but that she was "in there."

When I went home that night, I searched online for more information about lissencephaly. I finally found a reference about life expectancy that reported cases of patients living to 16 years old, and some had been known "to retain their intelligence." I was convinced, correctly or not, that Catherine was, indeed, "in there."

The next morning, I remembered that I wanted to write something in that Remembrance Book. Originally, I thought it might be a chore to think of something appropriate to say, but after our new connection the day before, I eagerly sat down in a quiet part of the unit to make my entry.

I thought back to all the years this child may have understood so much more than anyone thought possible, yet she was unable to speak. I thought about how she endured countless seizures, respiratory treatments, and the panic of not being able to breathe. Some very emotional words flowed naturally, as if I knew what to say all along.

I signed it, "Sweet Catherine, I am sending you my love." And then the words went blurry from my tears.

Justin and Sarah returned to the hospital later that day and thanked me for staying with Catherine. Justin pulled me aside and told me he had read what I wrote in the Remembrance Book and began talking about it. Immediately, I held up my hand, gesturing for him to stop, and he did. It was very emotional for me, and I think he clearly understood that, even without an explanation. What I wrote for Catherine was between the two of us. To this day, I have never spoken about the contents of my message to her, which is why I have consciously decided not to include it in this memoir.

A few days later, during my next shift at the hospital, darling Catherine passed away. Her parents, having lived in anticipation of this day for 17 years and, in the last week, knowing the end was imminent, handled her death with great dignity.

Justin asked me to go down to the lobby and inform the members of their church who had gathered in anticipation of this news. I approached a woman who I knew was the point person of the group. I put my arms around her and told her, "Catherine has gone to heaven." She cried quietly and hugged me for some time. I then brought her up to see Sarah and Justin.

During this shared grieving process, it was natural for people to speak openly about their most special moments with Catherine. I briefly debated whether or not to share my special moment with her and what I read about documented cases of children like Catherine "retaining intelligence." But I decided against it. There was no reason to bring up something so controversial at a time like this.

Instead, I kept it to myself along with my most precious memory of when Catherine and I stared so deeply into each other's eyes.

[16]

A Heavy Heart

NOT ALL OF THE PATIENTS are babies or young children. We had a patient named Shelby who was in her senior year in her high school's honors program. She was also an accomplished long distance runner and had already received several scholarships from highly regarded colleges.

Shelby was admitted to Children's with a newly diagnosed brain tumor and had surgery within a few days. The tumor was found to be benign with the expectation that she could be released within a week. The report was of great relief to her and her family.

I spoke with her mother, Tiffany, that afternoon, but neither of us realized that we would end up having many more conversations over the next several months.

Apparently, the tumor had been pressing up against her brain and, although benign, it had done more damage than originally thought. Shelby was confined to a wheelchair, unable to speak or walk, and she had respiratory problems. I don't think she was ever in a life-threatening condition, but it was certainly a very difficult time for her and the family.

I was in the PICU and NICU three days a week, and I visited with Tiffany just about every day I was there. She talked about Shelby's scholastic achievements, her running trophies, and, now, the fear and worry over what the coming days and months would bring.

Shelby remained in the PICU for several months, slowly improving. Tiffany slept in her room almost every night, even though she

My New Purpose

knew the nursing staff and respiratory therapists were providing thorough, quality care.

As time went by, I could see the situation was taking a toll on Tiffany. We had become close, and I treated her like a friend. I walked in one morning, and Tiffany looked exhausted. She clearly had not had a good night's sleep in weeks.

I told her she looked worn out and that she seemed to be losing weight. I was so concerned about her that I told her, in a stronger tone of voice than I would typically use with a parent, that I wanted her to go home, take a hot bath, have a glass of wine with dinner, and sleep in her own bed.

Tiffany listened to me and came in the next day looking a lot better.

As several months passed, Shelby was transferred to our rehabilitation unit. Although she showed progress, Tiffany shared with me that Shelby couldn't possibly accept most of her scholarships since the schools were simply too many hours away from home. There was also the issue of whether or not she could return to competitive running, which was such an important part of her life.

Two months later, Shelby was ready to be discharged. Still wheelchair-bound, she was stable enough to continue as an outpatient.

The time came to say our goodbyes, and I knew it would difficult for all of us. I first said goodbye to Shelby and wished her all good things in life. Then Tiffany and I walked into the hallway for more privacy. We hugged and Tiffany thanked me for everything. Her voice cracked, and I realized mine did, too. We finished and quickly parted ways, and I left the unit with a heavy heart.

I remember trying to get away without the nurses noticing me. This was the second time I had become so close, perhaps too close, to a patient and the family. The "saying goodbye" part wasn't getting easier.

[17]

It's Okay, Buddy

I WAS IN MY SEVENTH year at Children's Hospital when yet another DFACS child would touch my heart.

One morning in the PICU, a nurse named Julie came to me with a sense of urgency. She had a new DFACS admit she wanted me to go see.

Robbie was six years old and had experienced a lifetime of abuse and torture. When I went to see him, he was intubated with a breathing tube, but his sedation was being reduced in preparation for its removal. Many patients become agitated as they start to come out of sedation.

But so far, Robbie was doing well, and I spent some time softly talking to him, checking for a non-verbal response. After about 30 minutes, I asked him if I could hold his hand. Without hesitation, he moved his hand over and took my hand.

Julie happened to walk into the room, and when she saw him reach for my hand, it brought her to tears. As it turned out, everyone in the unit had become very attached to Robbie.

I came in every day that week and spent all of my time with him. Starting on the second day, I put him on my lap with his back against my chest and my arms wrapped around him, holding each of his hands in mine, and we'd sit by the front door. He needed love.

There were many different people on Robbie's treatment team, including physicians, nurses, respiratory therapists, social workers, x-ray techs, and more. Every time anyone came near the door of his room, Robbie would become very agitated, and his whole body would shake. Once, he yelled out to one of the nurses, "Don't hit me!" I would hold him and whisper in his ear, "It's okay, buddy. You're okay now."

Robbie started to improve during the next couple of weeks, and DFACS was working towards finding him a foster home. They made a connection with a young couple that had never fostered a child before, but somehow they had heard about Robbie and made some calls.

Robbie spent his last couple of weeks at the hospital in the rehab unit. When I heard that he was about to be discharged, I went to say goodbye. I said a few words to him then leaned over and kissed his forehead. Once again, I realized I needed to leave immediately while I still had my emotions barely under control.

[18]

No Fault of Their Own

IT MAY BE HARD TO imagine why working at the hospital with sick children would remind me of my working days as a businessman, but there was one thing that would trigger a connecting memory: children.

There was a time when our company became interested in going into a joint venture manufacturing arrangement with the biggest operation in Thailand. It was an opportunity that would greatly improve our market reach.

There were many meetings with lawyers and executives, but I realized there was something that could be a problem. I didn't want the manufacturer to use child labor in the plants that had our corporate name displayed, both from an ethical standpoint as well as the optics it could create.

I decided to bring up the subject at a private dinner with the manufacturing company's president, Pramod. He kind of smiled and said, "You have nothing to worry about, there will not be any child labor in these factories."

I told him I was glad to hear it, but I went on to ask him why he was smiling. Pramod was a fairly young man and was very respectful to me, so he hesitated for a moment before going on to explain that he thought people from America sometimes had a naïve view of what went on in other parts of the world. For instance, we might be surprised to know that in his country, for a 12-year-old girl who worked in a factory, the alternative was often child prostitution. He added that many men visit Bangkok from different parts of the world looking to have sex not with a "young girl" or a "teenage girl," but specifically with a "12-year-old girl."

It took me a few moments before I could start breathing again. I fully understood the dilemma but, bottom line, I still couldn't accept 12-year-old girls working six days a week behind a sewing machine in a hot factory.

I ended up retiring before the deal was done, but it soon came to fruition. The knowledge of how these poor young girls in Bangkok struggled never left me. Instead, I would find myself remembering them as I would meet sick children fighting to get well in the hospital. There are so many parts of the world where young girls are devalued, and these children, through no fault of their own, must struggle with a variety of bad options with low expectations.

[19]

My New Buddy

ONE OF THE OLDEST patients I ever dealt with at Children's Hospital was 18-year-old Lester. When I met him, he was being transferred to the TICU after spending the previous six months in the rehab unit.

Lester was on a ventilator and had significant respiratory issues caused by a series of medical problems. While he was mentally alert, he was unable to speak, but we would read his lips as he mouthed words.

There was going to be a meeting with Lester and his new care team in TICU, and I was asked to spend some time with him beforehand. We decided to play Yahtzee, a game I had to relearn every time I played it. It quickly became obvious that Lester was going to beat me badly, so I accused him of cheating. He got a big kick out of that, and it became clear that we would get along. Although he could not laugh audibly, Lester shook his head back and forth with this huge smile on his face. He could totally crack up, and he cracked me up in doing so.

It was time for Lester to join the meeting with his new team. When I pushed his wheelchair into the room, there was a crack in the floor with about a half-inch chunk of raised concrete, and I tripped. I leaned close to Lester's ear and whispered, "Wouldn't it be hysterical if I knocked you out of the wheelchair in front of all these people?" He "laughed" in the way he did with his big grin. We were now officially buddies.

My New Purpose

Lester was a challenging patient but also a sweet and considerate guy. Sometimes he asked me to watch one of his favorite TV shows, *The Walking Dead*, with him on his computer. He tried to put it at an angle that allowed me to fully view the screen and kept checking to make sure I could see it.

Lester required suctioning every 30 to 60 minutes and was known to need more attention from the nurses than most other patients.

Once, during my time with Lester, I decided to share a story from my days in the U.S. Army. I already knew that he grew up in a rough, inner-city neighborhood, and before he got sick, Lester had had a troubled past. So I thought he would like my story.

I began, "I grew up in the Bronx in a low-income area that was relatively peaceful except when kids got into fights. I had a few of them in school but, more often than not, my preference was to negotiate a peaceful settlement as an alternative to getting my ass kicked in." Lester was already cracking up.

I continued, "When I went into the Army, I went through 16 weeks of basic training in a heavy weapons infantry unit. Then the entire unit was shipped out to Korea and saw combat in the final four months of the Korean War."

I explained that, instead of shipping out, ten of us were assigned to the Presidential Honor Guard in Arlington, Virginia. I had to meet stringent criteria to be selected, including being a marksman. The unit was an easy assignment given what the rest of the guys were facing in Korea.

I told Lester about this one guy in our honor guard unit with whom I had a problem. I have no recollection why, other than the fact that he called me "Jew boy" and I called him "shithead" which, oddly, seemed to irritate him.

It became inevitable that we would come to blows someday, and that day finally arrived at 7:30 one morning. Words were said, and it was clear to both of us that it was time for us to "settle this right here and right now."

My New Purpose

Lester seemed to cling to my every word. "The company building was a U-shaped design with a concrete lot in the middle where we would normally fall out or line up every morning before breakfast. Shithead and I made our way there, and the entire company gathered around the windows of the building to watch the fight of the century."

Lester was still gripped, and I continued. "The gladiators stepped out to the lot. As I turned to face him, Shithead jumped me, wrapped his arm around my neck, and we fell to the ground. I didn't know it, but the moment we hit the concrete, Shithead broke his arm."

Lester was now rolling back and forth in his bed, smiling as broadly as he could, shaking his head. He couldn't believe my good fortune, but there was more, so I settled him down.

"Lester, wait a minute, the best is yet to come!" I said. "So we hit the ground, Shithead broke his arm, and I ended up on top of him. I grabbed the front of his shirt and, with my right fist, hit him with the greatest punch of my, albeit limited, violent career."

I told Lester he would have loved to see it in person. "Man, it was a fabulous punch! I hit him square in the face. Still, I was eager to finish the fight in case Shithead somehow regained his ability to end my life, so I cocked my right arm to punch him again…then pulled back when I noticed he didn't resist."

I continued, "It appeared that the fight had ended. So I theatrically pushed him in the chest and simply stared him down, then walked back to the barracks with confidence, totally uninjured. All of the guys were watching me with looks of respect."

Lester thought that was the end of my story, but I said, "Wait, there's more!" And that made Lester do his laugh once again.

"This is the best part!" I said. "Shithead went to the infirmary and returned two hours later with his arm in a cast and a sling, sporting a fantastic black eye that covered half of his face." Lester about fell out of his bed.

"The end of the story is that I, probably the most peaceful soldier in the U.S. Army, now enjoyed a new reputation. The word went out to the entire company and beyond, 'Don't fuck with Deutchman'!"

After some more laughter and banter, it was time for Lester to rest.

※

I soon learned Lester's case management team was figuring out his long-term plan. He required complex care, and although everyone seemed to love him, he was also considered to be a high-maintenance patient.

Appropriate placement was critical as the hospital had a strict cut-off age of 21. Although that was a couple of years away, it took a long time to find a place that a) would meet Lester's treatment needs, and b) be willing to take on the associated financial costs.

There was a facility in Florida that was looking good, and case managers discussed it with him. Lester became very excited about going there, but the whole plan fizzled when the facility declined to accept him because of its Medicaid budget.

Another six months went by and Lester's condition was declining. He had been at Children's Hospital for more than a year when one day, he simply closed his eyes and died.

My New Purpose

David in the U.S. Army, 1953, Fort Myer, VA.

[20]

"Trauma Houston"

USUALLY, WHEN PATIENTS CAME into the ICU, I became involved with the parents almost immediately.

A 17-year-old boy named Steve came into the hospital as "Trauma Houston" with severe traumatic injuries. When emergency crews brought in an unresponsive patient, he was assigned a name such as "Trauma Houston," "Trauma Seattle," or "Trauma Boston." It was a method used to maintain continuity and quality of care. Even when the hospital learned the patient's real name, he continued to be listed with his trauma name, again for continuity purposes.

I met Steve's father, Kevin, the first day Steve arrived. I learned he was very active and played on his high school lacrosse team. As the news of his accident spread amongst his friends, they came into the hospital to see him and to console his family.

There were so many of his friends in the PICU waiting room wanting to see Steve that they spilled into the hallways. They were sitting on the floor and began to create a security problem because they were blocking egress to and from the unit.

Soon it became apparent that Steve's injuries were not survivable. Kevin shared with me that the family had agreed to donate their son's organs, and at least six other children would be the recipients. Kevin was remarkably composed, given what he and his family were facing.

At some point, he mentioned that he once lived in the Bronx for a short time, and that his mother, Muriel, lived there for many years, ironically at the same time and on the same street where I lived as a child. It gave us an inherent "bond," and Kevin asked me if I would be willing to speak with his mother. Of course, I agreed.

Kevin brought me to the waiting room to introduce me to Muriel. There were at least 30 people crammed in there. Muriel greeted me with warmth and grace. She was a lovely woman, probably about the same age as me.

We chatted about the Bronx, where we went to high school, and some of the landmarks we both remembered. As we continued, I took her hands and told her how sorry I was that we had to meet under these circumstances. She nodded, quietly crying. I squeezed her hands, leaned even closer to her, and said softly, "Muriel, you have to get through this."

She nodded and said, still crying, "Yes, I know."

I kissed her on her cheek and turned to talk to Kevin's sister, who was standing next to us. Filled with emotion, she gave me a hug, and I left to go back to the unit.

Doctors had gathered in Steve's room to do some tests to determine his suitability as an organ donor. The charge nurse was about to go into his room, and she told me not to allow anyone in while this assessment was being done. A few of Steve's friends who had been waiting to see him had to be turned away. They were all in tears.

When the doctors finished, they asked me to find Steve's parents and bring them to the consult room. This was where serious conversations were held, typically between just the doctors and parents.

Kevin was in the hallway and I found Steve's mother in the waiting room. I escorted them quietly to the consult room.

It became clear to all those in the waiting room what had transpired. The friends began to leave, visibly shaken that they wouldn't have a chance to tell Steve goodbye.

[21]

Pink Sparkle Nail Polish

ONCE IN A WHILE we had a "miracle kid." I especially remember a four-year-old girl named Abby who came in with a traumatic brain injury, or TBI. A tree that was being cut down fell and struck her on the head. Her original prognosis was poor with concerns that she may not survive.

When I came in the following week, her condition had slightly improved. It looked like she would definitely live, but the big question was how much brain damage there was, and what would her quality of life be.

The following week, the moment I entered the unit, a nurse told me I must go see our "miracle kid." I practically ran in there and found Abby awake and alert, although still very weak. I couldn't believe the progress she had made in just a few days.

I asked her if there was anything she would like. She said very softly, "Do you have any pink sparkle nail polish?"

I said, "Sure, honey, I'll get you some." As I left the room, her nurse asked me if we really had any pink sparkle nail polish, and I said, "I have no idea, but if we don't, I'm driving over to Target to buy her some!" Believe me, Abby was going to have her pink sparkle nail polish.

So off I went on this very important mission. After checking a few places with no luck, I found myself in a small room that had mostly medical equipment, but also a couple of shelves with games and toys. As I sorted through them, I saw a plastic pail, like the type you take to the beach. It had a big sticker on it that read "nail polish." And inside, believe it or not, I found a bottle of pink sparkle.

I couldn't get back to Abby's room fast enough. She was so happy when I gave her the polish, and so was I. She asked me if I would paint her nails, but I told her I wasn't qualified.

I never knew from week to week what I would find in the ICU.

[22]

"Trachy" Moms

ON MANY OCCASIONS, I met a baby and his mother just a day or two after their arrival at Children's Hospital. This was the case with Ricky, who was just transferred into our TICU. One of Ricky's many medical problems made it impossible for him to breathe on his own, so he had a tracheostomy ("trach") and was on a ventilator.

Erika, Ricky's mother, used to come see her son often, but on Wednesdays, she couldn't get there until after 11:00 a.m. Wednesday was one of my regular days, so I got into the habit of holding their little boy before she arrived.

I got to know Erika's husband, Brady, who happened to be an avid sports fan. I always teased him when his team suffered a humiliating loss.

Some mornings Erika would bring her older son, Eli, who was about nine. Eli seemed to stay in the back of the room and not be included in the adult conversations.

I had seen this many times before and had developed a special interest in our patients' siblings over the years. Through no fault of their own, their lives were changed and, in many cases, would never be the same.

Eli was a sweet boy, so when the timing was appropriate, I made a point of taking him aside to talk with him. I asked him about school, his interest in sports, and his friends. I wanted to show him that we cared about him, too.

My New Purpose

As more time went by, Erika became friendly with two other moms in the TICU whose kids also had trachs and were on ventilators. They shared their fears and talked about the challenges ahead of them. These moms happened to all live in the same area and, as their friendships grew, they decided to form a support group for other moms who had kids with trachs.

They called themselves the "Trachy Moms." They had meetings with new moms in the TICU and tried to help calm their anxieties and fears. They met in the hospital cafeteria between the breakfast and lunch hours so they would just about have the place to themselves. They were a terrific group of strong, bright, young women.

After Ricky was discharged, Erika brought him in once in a while for follow-up tests. Each and every time, the TICU nurses were thrilled to see him and how he had thrived. I learned that he also had a new little brother, who I eventually got to meet.

When they came in, I got to catch up with Eli when he was with them, apart from the crowd that always gathered to see Ricky.

This was a family I would always remember and love. I hope life is good for them.

[23]

The Nurses

THERE ARE MANY REASONS why my 12 years at Children's has been so rewarding, and the nurses are one of them. Their warmth, humor, and friendships have been wonderful, an unexpected bonus of my volunteer work at the hospital. Even now, in my twelfth year, it's rare that I make it down a hallway in any of the units without at least one nurse giving me a warm hug to say hello.

I have become very close to a great many of them, mostly young women in different stages of their lives. Some have talked to me about their private lives, often about relationship issues and, sadly, more than a few divorces.

In one such instance, I was sitting with a baby sleeping in my arms when Bobbie, a young nurse who happened to be very pretty, approached me, seemingly upset. She told me she had just broken up with her boyfriend and felt like she had wasted three years of her life.

I tried to encourage her to reflect on the more meaningful aspects of their relationship and that, at one time, she did have feelings for this man.

"You haven't wasted three years of your life," I said. "And remember, you're young and smart, and you're not too ugly, so I don't think you have much to worry about!"

Bobbie gave me her signature smile and thanked me for being her pseudo-therapist.

My New Purpose

Sometimes we had babies in the NICU who were ready to be discharged and were no longer "connected" to anything. We liked to get those babies out of their cribs and carry them around.

One day I was holding one of them, and I sat down with her next to a nurse, Janie, who was about to give another baby a bottle. This was during a time of day we called "Quiet Time" when we lowered the shades, turned the lights down to be dimmer than usual, and spoke in a softer tone of voice.

Janie and I chatted for a while, each comforting our babies. She began telling me about her teenage years, her family, and her marriage. She spoke openly about some very personal issues, and I listened to her without saying a word. Without knowing it for certain, I got the feeling she was revealing things about herself that she had never shared with anyone else in the hospital.

We really didn't know each other that well and here we were, sitting together in this quiet, dark atmosphere sharing an intimate conversation. It was a sweet, tender moment.

So I not only got to hold babies but, in a certain way, I also became the ICU Dad.

[24]

My Little Girl

SOME OF OUR CHILDREN didn't have parents available to visit, make decisions, or advocate for them.

Six-year-old Kara, brought in by DFACS, suffered from multiple anomalies. The information we got about her family history was sketchy, and there was a lot we didn't know. The story, or at least my understanding of it, was that her brother went to school wearing what teachers described as "rags." When the boy stopped coming to school altogether, the teachers became concerned, which led to a multi-agency investigation.

When the police visited the home, they found a deplorable situation. The place was in shambles, and they found Kara lying in a bed in her feces and obviously malnourished.

It was a clear example that child abuse wasn't limited to kids being beaten or babies being shaken. It also applied to abandonment of care, failing to feed a child, change diapers, or provide any of the basic care we associate with having a child.

Kara was immediately transported to Children's and admitted to TICU for specialized care. I never heard what happened to her brother. After a few days of spending time with this sweet girl, I ended up getting involved with the doctors in a way I never did before or have since.

One of Kara's anomalies was a deformity of the tongue that impeded her ability to speak, swallow, drink, or eat.

After a few weeks of intensive care, Kara had gained some weight and stabilized. When she was a couple of weeks from being discharged, I learned that DFACS had arranged for her to stay in a foster home about 100 miles away. It was also determined that the problem with her tongue would be surgically repaired at a hospital near this new foster home.

I didn't like this plan because I thought the repair was relatively simple and should be done sooner and at our hospital. "Why wait?" I thought. So I decided to ask one of Kara's doctors about this, and although he heard me out, it became clear that the decision wouldn't change.

Two days later, I was in the TICU again and found another one of Kara's docs to ask him the same thing. It seemed so easy to fix, why would they wait? Why leave Kara with that problem for one more day?

I kept thinking about how greatly her life would change if and when she could eat, drink, swallow, and communicate better. I had the opportunity to speak to yet a third doctor and got the same result. The surgery would be done at another hospital at a later date.

I realized that I had no business getting involved to that degree, but I felt like an advocate for Kara and was therefore compelled to speak out. Certainly, she was getting great care, but I wanted to see her tongue get fixed. The doctors had their reasons for their decision, even if they weren't fully understood by me. After all, they were the docs.

Later that week, I saw the first doctor I spoke to about the issue. I was obviously annoyed and spoke with him in a tone I would rarely use with anyone, let alone a physician at the hospital. He ended up interrupting me and told me Kara's surgery was scheduled for one o'clock that day.

I was so relieved and happy. It seemed that my lobbying effort had paid off. This was my little girl.

[25]

"Pray for My Son"

WE HAD A 15-YEAR-OLD boy who was flown in from another city after being in a bad car wreck. The family was in a terrible state since their son had suffered a brain injury, and it wasn't yet known how much damage it had caused.

I found Mom and Dad in an atmosphere that was quiet and tearful. We spoke for a few minutes and, as I began to leave, the father walked out with me. I stopped at the door and asked him, "Is there anything at all I can do for you?"

He replied, "Yes. Pray for my son."

I hugged him, and he began to cry. At times like this, I search for anything I can say to console the parents. Many times there are just no words.

One week later, I saw Mom was alone in the room, and I went in to check on her. She told me they learned yesterday that their son did, in fact, suffer permanent brain damage. As I looked at her son, it was apparent from his behavior that he didn't know what he was doing.

I embraced her, and even though I knew her so briefly, I still found it difficult to say goodbye. I could only think of how vastly the lives of this entire family would be forever changed.

I really hated the car wrecks. While we had to accept that there would be a certain number of children who would develop a brain tumor or suffer acute respiratory failure, or babies might come into the NICU with any one of a dozen different syndromes, the kids getting injured in car wrecks were completely healthy a moment before impact.

I guess I've seen too many broken bodies and too many broken-hearted moms and dads.

[26]

Don't Forget Mom

I HATE THINKING ABOUT when I feel like I've screwed up, even though this has only happened a few times. There were two cases that would particularly bother me.

There was a boy about 16 years old who was in and out of our TICU. Joey had the sweetest smile that everyone noticed. He spent a lot of time on his computer, connecting with friends on social media. He wasn't able to speak, and although we could communicate to a degree, the situation wasn't conducive to a very long visit.

Joey's mom would often be in his room, and we would briefly chat, but I didn't make a deliberate attempt to get to know her as I did with so many other moms. I could make excuses, such as I needed to spend time with a critical patient or visit a new admit, but I knew better. At best, it was careless of me.

Joey was back in the PICU, and it became obvious that things had changed. He was alone in the room, which was dark, he wasn't on his computer, and he looked afraid. I asked if he wanted me to come in for a visit. He emphatically nodded his head "yes." I put on a gown, mask, and gloves since he was on "contact precautions," and sat down next to him.

I held his hand and talked with him. It was obvious he was in great distress, which I found alarming since I had never seen him like that. I learned he was declining rapidly.

Ten minutes after I left him, Joey died. His parents were notified earlier to come to the hospital but were unable to make it before he passed. When they arrived, I stood aside, feeling terrible, not only because Joey had died, but because I never extended myself to his mom. In so many other cases, I offered some comfort to the family. I felt like I had let this mom down. I also had deep regrets that I wasn't there still holding Joey's hand when he took his final breath.

Soon, I found myself in a similar situation.

We had a teenage boy named Chris who was also in and out of the hospital. Whenever I saw him, he was lying motionless on his bed, his mother by his side.

I learned from my regrets with Joey and his mother and I decided that, this time, I would make a deliberate effort to develop a relationship with Mom.

One morning I found Chris back in the PICU. His mother, Lucy, was there, sitting in the corner with the lights off. I asked if I could join her, and she nodded and gave me a welcoming smile. I offered her an immediate apology, and she looked confused since we had no previous interaction. I explained that I had seen her many times in the hospital, but I had never extended myself as I usually did with other parents.

Lucy quickly reassured me and said she was glad to meet me now. We chatted for a while. Despite the strain, worry, and demands of taking care of a special needs teenage boy, she had a calm demeanor and was charming and friendly.

I would see Lucy time after time, never knowing the details of her son's condition and never asking. After several months went by, I never saw Chris or Lucy again. But I was glad that I had paid attention to Mom.

[27]

Moments

MANY THINGS COULD HAPPEN in a moment of time. Sometimes they happened when I didn't know the patient or the family but, in any event, they have remained in my memory ever since.

One morning in the PICU, I saw two women holding up a third outside the waiting room. She was a young mom who was in obvious distress.

I asked them if they needed any help. They explained that she was in a serious car accident and her five-year-old son had died on the scene. Her three-year-old daughter was now in surgery. She didn't want to leave the hallway because she wanted to be sure she could see her little girl when they brought her back from surgery.

I was concerned that Mom might faint at some point and injure herself. I explained that there was no way to know how long her baby could be in surgery. I then offered to bring them to a private room, but they declined, so I located our chaplain and let her handle it.

This all transpired in no more than a couple of minutes yet that mother's face, cringed with anguish and horror, was etched into my memory.

I didn't meet this next patient, but I did meet her father. A three-year-old girl was very sick in the PICU and her father was outside her room, being comforted by some friends.

A company had sent up trays of food for families in-unit, as happened every so often. I asked the dad if he had eaten anything today, and he said no. When I tried to encourage him to eat something, he explained that he just couldn't bring himself to eat.

I put my hands on his shoulders and said, "It's okay, it's okay," not unlike what I said to the babies I held.

He leaned into my arms and cried. I held him there until he let go.

My first prayer.

Children's has chaplains in each of the ICUs as well as other areas of the hospital. They play an important role when families go through difficult times. There are also times when a family has asked their own preacher to visit them in the hospital to see their child.

One day I was in the NICU and noticed a family gathered around a baby. The baby was admitted two weeks earlier with life-threatening problems that couldn't be treated, and she wasn't expected to make it through the day.

I walked over and stroked the side of her head and said, "Oh, baby." The baby's mother, grandma, and aunt looked on.

I gave them my condolences and the grandma asked me if I would say a prayer for their baby. The chaplain was on the other side of the unit, so I felt compelled to honor her request, although I had never said a prayer in front of other people.

The four of us joined hands in a small circle, heads bowed, tears already running down their cheeks as I began. "Dear Lord, please take this baby in your arms and hold her close to your heart. Drive the pain and fear from her little body and, please Lord, hold her hand on her journey to heaven. Amen."

Once in a while I would be assigned to the front desk, which would almost always be more interesting than I expected.

Every so often, a woman in labor would walk in, ready to give birth any minute. They were supposed to go to a hospital one block away, so we would call for a bus (ambulance) to get them over there.

When I asked them why they came here instead of the birthing hospital, some would say, "Your sign said Children's Hospital and I'm having a child."

I met a six-year-old boy in PICU named Jayden who asked to play with some Play-Doh. I found a few cans of it, and we both played with it, making different things.

I rolled a piece of it like a cigar but, instead of pretending to smoke it, I placed it on the right side of my nose and made believe it was a snake crawling up my nose. I was acting like I was falling off my chair because, after all, the snake was almost coming out of my ear. Jayden was laughing hysterically. A nurse walked in because of the commotion and kind of told me I was crazy.

Sadly, Jayden died about six months later. On the anniversary of his death, his mom came to the PICU with presents for the kids.

Another boy in PICU, Ryan, was 11 years old and lonely. Since he was blind, when I walked into his room, I announced my entrance and introduced myself.

After we talked for a while, I asked him if I could hold his hand. He immediately held his hand out in search of mine. Ryan had just been admitted when a nurse came in to tell him he was going to be transferred to another room. Ryan became agitated, so I offered to stay with him. As the nurse wheeled his gurney from one hallway to the next, Ryan kept asking, "David, are you still there?"

"Yes, buddy, I'm still here," I said, and he smiled.

After he got settled in his new room, I held his hand again, and he began talking about his past. He told me he hoped I could meet his foster mom because she was so nice. He added, "My birth mom was never nice to me."

I gently squeezed Ryan's hand, and he put his other hand on top of mine. And then, unexpectedly, I felt my eyes welling up.

Ryan was a sweet boy who clearly had limited happiness in his life.

The oncology unit called me to ask if I could help watch a patient and his brother while the doctors met with their parents. Johnny and Jose were watching television when I arrived, so I figured this was going to be an easy assignment.

Then Johnny, who was the cancer patient, said he had to go potty. Since he had a couple of lines hooked up to him, he couldn't get to a toilet.

His brother, Jose, seemed familiar with the situation and said he knew what to do. He instructed me to put some gloves on and he went to grab "the pee bottle."

Johnny seemed to know the drill, too, and he stood up on the bed and pulled his pants down. Jose said, "Now, you have to hold it for him."

"I'm not holding it," I said "You hold it, you're his brother."

"I don't want to hold it, you do it," he said.

"That's not in my contract!"

As this drama was going on, three Child Life women walked into the room, and I said, smiling, "Excuse us, Johnny is peeing."

They left us, also smiling, and we shared a laugh later when I told them the story.

My New Purpose

Family conflicts and dynamics that happened outside of the hospital many times made their way in, and I often found myself in the middle. This was the case with a 16-year-old girl in PICU who was dying. Her parents were divorced but both were in the room. Suddenly, the mom started screaming, "My baby, my baby!"

Dad ran out of the room and a nurse ran in, and a chaplain quickly followed. I went into the hallway where Dad had gone. He was leaning against a window, alone, sobbing terribly. It was upsetting to see that at certainly the most tragic moment of their lives, these two parents couldn't put the anger and animosity aside and come together.

Sometimes we had sick children who weren't expected to live and there was a sibling who wasn't aware of the severity of the situation. In one case, the parents of a three-year-old girl who had died asked one of our Child Life specialists, Lexi, for assistance in telling their eight-year-old son.

Lexi had specific training on how to talk to children about death and dying. She took the boy into a private room and explained to him, in an age-appropriate manner, exactly what had happened, and that his little sister had died. The parents were grateful.

When a baby passed away, a Child Life specialist asked the mother if she wanted a mold of her baby's hand as a remembrance. Sometimes they did a mold of the mother's hand holding her baby's hand. It was presented to the mother in a white box with a pink or blue ribbon with intentions for the parents to display it in their home.

I will never forget the mothers I saw taking that keepsake home instead of their baby.

[28]

You're Hired!

YOU WON'T BELIEVE IT, but the hospital hired me as an employee at the age of 79!

It was September 2013, eight years after becoming a volunteer, when I learned about a "PRN," an "as-needed" position. There were about half-a-dozen PRNs in the group covering various assignments in the Emergency Department, including the ICU, PCA, front desk, etc.

Hannah, the manager, was in favor of my coming onboard, but she was also very candid about the requirements. Specifically, she emphasized the demands of a 12-hour shift in the ED, 1:00 p.m. to 1:00 a.m.

One of the other PRNs told me that he had never been asked to do an ED shift and, instead, did all of his shifts in other units with a different, and easier, schedule. I thought perhaps I, too, would spend most of my time in other units, but even so, I felt I could handle the ED shifts, and I assured her that I was willing and able to do it.

In a final meeting with Hannah and Brandi, the supervisor in the ED, I was hired. And that's when I realized I was actually hired specifically for the ED, although I took some shifts in other units as well.

I spent my first few weeks in orientation and then worked a few shifts in PICU to cover for someone taking a vacation. My primary job was to meet with new admissions in the three ICUs to check on the parents, help get them anything they needed, and make them aware of the hospital facilities that were available for families.

It was similar to what I had done as a volunteer but with a broader scope, so I was even more involved. For instance, in addition to checking the census and new admits, I was included in "rounds." These daily morning meetings started when the charge nurse had all of the latest information assembled and included a detailed review of each patient in the PICU. These were detailed conversations with nothing held back or minimized. I was now included in these team discussions to plan care for our patients.

One morning before rounds, I visited a new admit. Mom, while upset, was basically okay. Dad, on the other hand, was a wreck.

At the rounds meeting later that morning, when that patient's case came up, I mentioned to the chaplain what I had witnessed. The chaplain told me she would be sure to visit that family first.

Another time there was a discussion about a parent who was verbally abusive to the staff, yelling, cursing, and threatening them. It was strongly suggested we all stay out of that room unless it was medically necessary.

Sometimes I went into the room anyway, and I did so in this case. I was clearly the oldest guy in the unit, and I found that when I approached this mom, she was at ease with me. I spent 30 minutes with her, and it became a lovely conversation.

The next day we saw each other in the lobby, and she came over to hug me. I had made a new, though unlikely, friend.

I especially enjoyed my liaison work in the ICU since I knew all of the staff and was comfortable there. Often, ICU patients are hospitalized for an extended period, and I spent a lot of time with these parents over weeks and sometimes months.

In more acute emergencies, for instance in the ED, my interaction with parents was often fast and focused. One afternoon, Brandi was escorting about a dozen family members from the ED up to the waiting room in PICU. The chaplain was there, and so was I. A woman and her two children were in a bad motor vehicle accident, and the kids were seriously injured.

The ten-year-old boy was still being stabilized in the trauma unit, but the three-year-old girl was expected to arrive in PICU from the ED very soon. Usually they would stop by the waiting room so that the parents could briefly see their child, but with this patient, that was not the case. Staff wanted to get her into her room and settled as quickly as possible.

The little girl, Megan, was brought into her room. It was an active and complicated scene, so I stayed to make myself available for any needs that came up.

Megan had multiple traumatic injuries to the head, chest, and abdomen. She was intubated, and it took an hour to hook up her lines and get her settled. The goal now was to keep her stabilized and maintain a calm and quiet atmosphere in the room.

Still, we wanted to allow her father to see her, and when one of the nurses asked me to bring him in, and only him, I went to the waiting room.

I saw Dad at the front of the waiting room and told him he could come with me to see his daughter, but just him. A few of the grandparents quickly came up to me and asked if they could come as well. I told them only Dad for now, but I would come back for them as soon as I got the green light from the nurses.

Before I could leave with Dad, a woman ran up and literally jumped on me! She threw her arms around my neck, wrapped one of her legs around my leg and was totally off the floor, crying, "I'm the grandma, I'm the grandma! Please take me back with you, please."

At this point, I was considering my options of what to do. Should I ask Dad to help calm her down? Did I need to call security? Or I could let her come back with us, which is what I reluctantly did.

While we were sensitive to the anguish of the family, ultimately our patient was the priority. If it was in her best interest to keep guests to one at a time to help maintain that calm and quiet atmosphere, that was what should happen.

When Dad and Grandma entered the room and first saw Megan, it was understandably an emotional moment for both of them.

But while Dad maintained his composure, Grandma did not. She sobbed and held onto the bed railing, and I was concerned that she might fall and injure herself. Then she attempted to hug Megan, which—with all of her tubes and traumatic injuries—was dangerous. Fortunately, a nurse was right there and immediately intervened. The visit was over, and I was left wishing I had only brought Dad back with me.

A couple of hours later, Megan's brother, Kevin, came up to the floor, and he was in even worse condition and would remain in PICU long after Megan was moved to the rehab unit.

After a couple of months, Megan was ready to be discharged and her dad came to the PICU to thank the nurses for all their help. When I saw her, I got down on my knees and asked Megan if I could give her a hug. She ran to me with a giant smile and gave me one of the best hugs I have ever had.

[29]

Bring the Baby Back, Stat

BACK IN THE EMERGENCY Department, my orientation for that unit was underway. The training would involve three days and three nights. They gradually increased the number of hours I worked from an initial five hours to what would be 12.

My first day, I was assigned to shadow the senior supervisor for the unit. It was only a five-hour shift, from 1:00 to 6:00 p.m. There was a lot to learn, and I found there were many things specific to the ED I'd have to become familiar with.

I began by learning the physical layout of the department, the different classifications of rooms for the various patients waiting to be seen, and the procedure for bringing patients from the waiting room to a treatment room.

Wait time was inherent in our system, and I quickly learned it was a big issue for worried parents. While many became impatient and expressed frustration, at times I dealt with parents who were beyond irritated and angry.

The next shift, from 1:00 to 9:00 p.m., was much more interesting because the ED was substantially more hectic after six o'clock. The assessment nurse was the first one to see new arrivals, and she triaged each patient by assigning a color. You may be familiar with "Code Blue," the very highest priority and a designation that meant the patient wasn't breathing. "Code Red" indicated a very high acuity level, and then there were three other levels of priority.

I learned that perhaps 70% of the patients who came through our ED did not, in fact, even need to be there. But the other 30% absolutely did. Of that first group, there were some mothers who were "regulars" who often tried to demand a code for their child to be seen sooner.

We had fast-track rooms for patients who could be seen and treated quickly and "not sick" rooms for injured kids to keep them from being exposed to sick and potentially contagious patients. The trauma rooms, only assigned by the charge nurse, were reserved for more seriously injured patients who usually arrived by ambulance or on a life-flight helicopter.

After my third and final day of training, from 1:00 p.m. to 1:00 a.m., I began one of my first shifts unsupervised. I studied the waiting rooms and was amazed to find how quickly I could tell whether a patient was sick, not sick, injured, or not injured.

I remember one patient on that shift who was running around the waiting room, saying to her mother, "Momma, look, they have a soda machine!" My newly acquired medical assessment skills told me, "This kid is going to be okay."

About ten minutes later, the charge nurse was notified that a life-flight was bringing in a five-year-old male with serious trauma who was not breathing. The medical staff was alerted and began to prepare for the imminent arrival of this critical patient.

Docs, nurses, respiratory, radiology, and half-a-dozen additional support staff appeared within 30 seconds. Soon, the flight nurses came in, quickly wheeling the patient's gurney into the trauma room. Everyone immediately went into action, each having a specific job to do. Although there was a clear sense of urgency, there was also a calm efficiency.

The patient's parents arrived simultaneously and went directly into the trauma room where staff was trying to resuscitate their child. We are trained for cases like this, and so without being directly told, I went to the parents and told them that I needed to take them

My New Purpose

to a private room to allow the doctors to do their jobs, and that they would come give them a report just as soon as they could.

They seemed to understand and almost expected that they would be asked to leave. Once I got them to a private waiting room, they seemed relieved not to be witnessing the terrifying scene in the trauma. Ten minutes later, doctors reported to the parents that their child was stabilized. By then, I was back in the ED dealing with other patients.

Each time I walked into the waiting rooms, which was about every 20 minutes, I saw parents trying to make eye contact with me. One couple had just arrived with their baby and the mother saw me, then quickly opened the child's shirt to reveal a massive scar from her neck to below her abdomen. The mother explained that the baby had had open-heart surgery at Children's just after birth and now had RSV (a common but often serious respiratory virus). The child was running a high temperature.

I told her to give me a minute, and I ran back to inform the charge nurse who quickly assigned a room and had me bring the baby back, stat. This was the first time I was that assertive with the charge nurse, and it turned out to be the right call. I was glad to begin to earn credibility in a new department.

When I returned to the waiting room, I learned that my actions had created a situation with racial undertones. Apparently there was an African-American mother who had been waiting with her child much longer than this other mom and her baby, who were white. The nurse told me she had complained and asked me to talk to her.

I was expecting to have a battle on my hands, but the moment I approached this mom, she was so sweet and just wanted to ask me a few questions. Once I explained the concept of "triage" to her, she immediately understood. In any event, I made sure her child was the next patient seen.

My New Purpose

But it didn't always work out that way. Sometimes we had a parent scream or curse and it got quite contentious. For that, and other reasons, we had a uniformed state trooper in the ED.

Later that night, I noticed a rather large man in the waiting room displaying threatening body language. He kept looking at his watch and shaking his head. I'm a big believer in diffusing a potentially bad situation rather than waiting for it to blow up, so I went over to sit down next to this man. I asked him if he had been waiting a long time to be seen.

He said yes, but in a calmer tone than I expected. I explained that, at that moment, he could only see the patients in the waiting room, but he couldn't see how many were coming in via ambulances or life-flights. It was these critical patients who required a lot of manpower in the treatment areas. He completely understood and seemed to quickly calm down.

Working in a children's hospital, there were many times I witnessed sadness, heartbreak, and loss. And sometimes there were little things unrelated to a patient's condition that would tug on my heart.

The ED saw Medicaid patients on a regular basis. Many of the families don't have access to transportation, so Medicaid would provide a car and driver to help them get to the ED and then back home. The process wasn't entirely seamless and, many times, these families had to wait as long as two to three hours for their rides.

I noticed, in every case, how the children sat patiently with a coloring book we had given them and didn't complain. I never heard them say to their mom, "I have nothing to do. I'm hungry, I'm thirsty, I'm bored." Not a word.

Oftentimes, there were as many as a dozen kids and their parents waiting for their rides back home, presumably hungry. We maintained a small supply of sandwiches and fruit to give out to these families but sometimes we ran out, and I would go down

My New Purpose

to the kitchen to get more. If there wasn't anymore, which happened from time to time, the kids didn't eat. And still, they didn't complain.

Just as I was always particularly sensitive about the DFACS kids, I felt the same way with these Medicaid children. They reminded me of me.

[30]

All in One Night

A FEW WEEKS LATER, on my first ED shift on my own, some nurses decided to "welcome" me. One of them asked me to go get a breast pump. There was a "pumping room" in NICU for new moms, so I didn't question the request. Off on my first mission I went, to find a breast pump.

When I got to the room where I thought I would find it, I had to ask the nearest nurse which piece of equipment was the breast pump. I brought it back to the nurse who requested it, and she smiled as two other nurses were cracking up. I laughed with them and asked if I had passed their test, and I had. It was a fun beginning to my first day in the ED.

The afternoons were relatively quiet, but I had enough tasks to keep me busy. It got busier around seven o'clock, including a few kids with sports-related injuries, mostly broken legs, from after-school games. Typically these were not serious injuries, but there was one ten-year-old boy who needed surgery.

When I walked into his room, his dad was sitting slightly behind him, so he couldn't see his son's face. The father announced that his son was waiting to have surgery and that he needed to "man up" and "be tough." What I saw was a terrified boy with tears in his eyes and a quivering lip.

I took the boy's hand in mine and explained how important the surgery was so that his leg would be as strong as it was before his injury. He nodded as if he understood, but I still saw the fear in his eyes. And when his father again gave him the "man-up" crap, I thought, "Give the kid a break." But, of course, I kept this to myself, and when I finally left them, the boy was still in despair.

A few minutes later, I visited a young girl who came in with her parents and grandmother. Unfortunately, I entered at a bad time, and Grandma went into attack mode immediately. She apparently was unhappy with her granddaughter's care, and she didn't like the doctor. I told her I was sorry she wasn't happy. I tried to assure her that we had quality physicians and staff, and that her granddaughter was in good hands. She seemed to calm down a bit, and as I left, I told them I would check back soon.

I visited a few other patients and then, as I walked past a treatment room, a physician stopped me. She asked me to get that patient's nurse. She explained that she had to examine this boy's penis and needed another person in the room. I was able to find her immediately, another task completed.

Five minutes later a cop walked in, pushing—at first appearance—a teenage girl in a wheelchair. Upon further review, I realized that she was handcuffed to the wheelchair. I asked a nurse what was going on, and she explained that sometimes patients come in from a juvenile jail facility.

I then went to sneak my third piece of a cinnamon crumb cake a doctor had brought in before I moved on to the next patient.

I walked through the waiting room to see if there were any pending issues or questions from parents. I saw a young couple enter the ED with a baby as pale as a ghost. The assessment nurse immediately responded and directed me to stand by. She got the baby processed and I brought them to a trauma room in less than one minute, when the doctors and nurses immediately began their assessment. That was my cue to escort the parents to the waiting room.

The father was a military man and easy to deal with, but the mother didn't want to leave her baby. A compromise was reached,

My New Purpose

and the two of them waited outside the room in the hallway until the doctor could come and brief them.

This situation was problematic because a) there couldn't be a chair in the hallway because it would block access to other rooms and b) with parents standing and in distress, there was the danger that one of them could pass out and injure themselves.

I again tried to take them to a consult room just down the hall, but Mom wouldn't leave that door. About 15 minutes later, the doctor emerged with his report. He calmly explained that the baby's heart was slightly irregular and that she needed to be admitted into the ICU. Mom seemed to jump three feet and said, alarmed, "You're taking her to Intensive Care?" The doctor explained some of the medical reasons why, and I tried to reassure her that it was best for their baby.

By now it was about 10:30 p.m., and I made yet another swing through the waiting room. I saw a baby with his parents, and Mom looked worried. I sat down next to her and asked what brought them to the ED that night. She explained that he was okay until he fell asleep, and then he would stop breathing. She said this kept happening, so she brought him to the ED. I told her I would be right back.

In this case, my experience in the NICU proved invaluable. I had held many babies there who would "brady," meaning they were having an episode of "bradycardia apnea." Here, the baby's heart rate would slow down so much that he would stop breathing.

NICU babies are hooked up to monitors, so when this happens there, alarms go off, a nurse yells, "He's bradying!", and staff rushes in to stabilize the baby.

I ran back to the charge nurse and, with a clear sense of urgency, told her I had a baby "bradying" in the waiting room. Without hesitation, she told me to get him back immediately to a trauma room, which I did. Everything worked out, and I had a sense of satisfaction that my eight years of experience in the NICU was proving useful.

My New Purpose

By the time it was 11:30 p.m., I was dragging but still checking on a few new patients. I left at 1:00 a.m., more exhausted than I had been in years.

[31]

One Final Wave

THERE WERE PLENTY OF cases where I visited with a critical patient one day only to learn that he was no longer there the next. And though I knew not to inquire about the condition of our patients, this was always a curious situation for me. Was the patient discharged, transferred to another unit, or had he passed?

I remembered that the Child Life representative had warned me early on not to go "falling in love with these kids." And I didn't, until I did. This is how it happened.

During a week when I was working in the ICU, I met a ten-year-old boy named Ethan. He had been treated for five years for medulloblastoma, a very common type of brain tumor in children. Other health issues had brought him from oncology to the ICU, and it appeared that Ethan's status was now becoming end-stage.

When I met Ethan, he was extremely frail, not talking, and barely moving. I quietly asked him if he would like some books from our library so I could read to him. He barely had the strength to nod "yes."

I pulled a chair as close to his bed as I could and lowered the railing. I leaned in close to him and, without him actually "moving," he seemed to nudge himself a little closer to me.

I think he enjoyed my reading to him, and when I finished the second book, I held his hand, feeling close to him. It was clear that

My New Purpose

he was too tired to continue, and I told him I would come back the next day and read to him again.

Ethan was clearly too weak to answer verbally or even with a smile...but he didn't have to. I knew during our short reading session that he would want me to come back. And I would.

I passed by his room a couple of times later that day, giving him a warm smile and a friendly wave. Somehow he was able to wave back at me, albeit very slowly. His mother told me that he didn't wave to anyone else. She said to me, through teary eyes, "He must really like you."

As the next few weeks went by, I made it a point to visit Ethan, no matter what my assignments were that day. Soon, I started to read to him with my arm around his shoulder so we would have our connection without requiring him to move. Ethan and I also continued to wave to each other when I passed by, a simple act that somehow spoke volumes.

This continued for nearly two months, and I began to realize I was becoming emotionally closer to Ethan than I should. One morning at a PICU rounds meeting, I arrived at the same time as Liza, an occupational therapist, before anyone else. I confided to her that I had become more emotionally connected with Ethan than I had with previous patients, despite my better judgment. I knew I wanted to be caring and giving, but there was an emotional boundary we all needed to respect.

Liza was a good listener, but there wasn't a good solution. She left me with that warning I had heard before, many times, "Don't go falling in love with the kids."

During my next shift in the PICU, I learned that Ethan was transferred back to the oncology department, so I went down there to see him. It was obvious that his condition had further declined. I spoke to his mother, but I respected their privacy and didn't pry for more information. Ethan was lying on his side, and I sat down next to him. I whispered that I didn't think this was a good time to read to him, but I wanted to visit him.

Ethan didn't answer with a nod. Instead, he slowly leaned his failing body closer to me. I gently put my hand on his back. It was the closest I could get to actually hugging him. Minutes seemed to pass, and I found myself frozen, unable to leave him, but very much needing to. When I walked out the door, we exchanged one final wave.

I was staying busy with other units and spent a few weeks covering the PCAs. What I'm trying to say, or perhaps find an excuse for, was that I never saw Ethan again.

A few months later, I learned that he had died. His obituary included dozens of notes of sympathy, prayers, remembrances, and photos. There was a picture of Ethan dressed up, smiling proudly at his kindergarten graduation. It was captioned "Five Months before Ethan's Diagnosis." I stared at this picture of that darling boy for a long time, and that's when I fell apart. I don't know how long I cried, but when I was finally able to compose myself, I vowed that I would never again allow myself to "fall in love with a kid."

[32]

Back to the ICU

BEFORE BECOMING A LIAISON, I spent eight years volunteering in the various intensive care units of Children's Hospital. The ICU was my home, and I loved it. I had built many meaningful relationships with the doctors and nurses, and I always felt welcome.

Now, as a liaison, I was working as many ICU shifts as I could get. My shift was usually 8:00 a.m. to 4:00 p.m., a few more hours than I was doing as a volunteer. But I noticed an impact stamina-wise three or four hours into my day. Although I enjoyed the more challenging aspects of my new job responsibilities, my energy level was becoming a problem.

I was also getting multiple requests to work the 12-hour ED shifts, and while I was trained for and agreed to this work, I was finding it almost impossible to do. Furthermore, my wife was worried about my working that many hours and coming home after midnight. So I found myself in a real dilemma.

I decided to speak with my supervisor to propose an eight-hour shift (3:00 p.m. to 11:00 p.m.), which would cover the busiest times. Although she was sympathetic to my situation, changing my hours was not an option, she explained, as it would set a precedent she didn't want established.

While I understood, I began taking fewer shifts overall, and none in the ED. I became concerned about my loss of energy and, ultimately, after much thought, I resigned from my liaison job after six months and returned to my volunteer position in the ICUs.

Just one week later at a doctor's appointment, a nurse taking my vital signs found that I had a very low heart rate, right around 40 beats per minute. Anything lower than 60 is considered bradycardic, or low. She suggested I see my cardiologist.

Within a week I had an angiogram, which proved normal, but I needed a pacemaker to get my heart beating at the right rate, regularly. The pacemaker worked immediately, increasing my rate from 40 to 70 beats per minute, and my energy level improved dramatically.

I only wish I had had an opportunity to work an ED shift with my new pacemaker and new-found energy. In any event, I was grateful for the opportunity and loved being a PRN, but I was also happy to be back in the ICUs as a volunteer.

[33]

My Babies

I WOULD HAVE TO SAY that holding babies is my specialty. It's what I most enjoy doing and it's what the babies need the most.

Over my 12 years at Children's, I estimate I have held roughly fourteen hundred babies in the NICU and sometimes in the PICU. I would like to say that I remember all of them, but I can honestly say I do remember many of them.

One of these babies was about two months old and had been abused. The charge nurse told me he was a DFACS baby, and I knew I wanted to hold him. The police had been in and out of his room, but there was no sign of his mother or her boyfriend.

I gently picked up that little guy and held him close. He fell asleep almost immediately, and a few minutes later, a woman came in and introduced herself as Charlotte, the baby's grandmother. Charlotte was a retired nurse and clearly distraught over the whole situation.

At one point a young woman walked in, spoke briefly to Charlotte, looked lovingly at the baby, then left. A few minutes later another woman walked in, and she, too, spoke briefly to Charlotte but didn't acknowledge the baby, then left.

I said to Charlotte, "That was the baby's mother, right?" She said she was but seemed baffled, and asked me how I knew.

I hesitated to answer until she suddenly became upset and repeated, "How did you know she was the mom?"

"Because she never looked at the baby," I said.

Near tears, Charlotte's head sunk as she shook it back and forth.

My New Purpose

It was only because of my past experiences with so many abused babies that I saw that as a universal sign. At the same time, I'm not suggesting that this mother participated in the abuse or knew anything about it, but the behavior was ominous.

It stands out when mothers don't ask to hold their babies or even look at them. After all, how could a mother not want to hold her baby, especially after learning he was abused?

Another baby, a one-month-old little girl, was abandoned, dehydrated, malnourished, and near death when she was brought into the ED by the police. She weighed just over two pounds.

When babies are admitted into the NICU without a known name, they are called Baby Girl or Baby Boy. I met little Baby Girl one day later in the NICU when the charge nurse told me that she would be my "primary," code for my number one responsibility for the day.

Holding her was like holding a little kitten. She was pathetically tiny, and she didn't move much or even cry. I would hold that sweet angel for hours every time I was in the NICU.

Several weeks later, Baby Girl had doubled her weight. I learned that a foster home had been identified for her, and I met her foster dad when he came in to handle the paperwork and I was holding her. I quickly nicknamed him "Mr. Wonderful," but not why you may think.

Picture this: I was holding Baby Girl for an hour as Mr. Wonderful was standing three feet away from me, clearly finished filling out forms. Staff was in and out of her pod, commenting on how adorable Baby Girl was, and not once did this guy even look at the baby. The baby's nurse was clearly unsettled by his detachment, and we exchanged a silent but communicative glance. We were both not feeling too good about this.

I made my feelings known to the baby's doctor, the charge nurse, and anyone I could find who was associated with Baby Girl's care. Her nurse did the same. But everything was already set in motion, and there were other factors that needed to be considered, of which neither of us were aware.

We had a very busy NICU with 35 beds, and there were new arrivals almost every day. Sometimes a baby was transferred to the PICU or TICU or, if the baby was stable enough, he or she would go to a room in the PCA.

In this case, Baby Girl was healthy enough to leave the hospital entirely and we had a qualified foster family ready to go. This was always the best outcome, even though I worried it might not be her best outcome.

Three-month-old Katie was flown in from a rural part of the state. Born premature, she had multiple problems, including spina bifida. I met Lacy, her teenage mother, within a few days after their arrival, and it was the beginning of what would be a year-long relationship. With Lacy there 95% of the time, Katie endured one emergency after another. It was a roller coaster, with mostly a downhill ride. Whenever I asked Lacy how she was doing, she would inevitably talk only about Katie.

One day I took her hand, looked into her eyes, and asked, "Lacy, how are you doing?"

She paused momentarily and then began telling me about her boyfriend, who was Katie's father. In all of these months, he had never visited his baby. Lacy explained that sometimes she felt like she was 19 years old going on 40, and that her boyfriend was 19 going on 16. Lacy clearly had a lot of obstacles ahead.

In another sad case, we had a baby born prematurely to a woman who used methamphetamines during her entire pregnancy. The baby was not only six-weeks premature, she was also addicted to meth.

My New Purpose

I arrived for my NICU shift the day after the baby was born and was quickly met by the charge nurse, who would make Lily my primary for the day.

Lily weighed less than three pounds and spent nearly all of her first 24 hours screaming. I picked her up and started to try everything to help her as I stroked the side of her head. I was finally able to calm her down and held her for two more hours.

I found it was helpful to try calming babies by the way I spoke to them and the way I held them. I always whispered to them, "It's okay, baby. Shhhh, you're okay." Sometimes I sang to them, but not the usual fare. I sang show tunes, sometimes a little Beatles, and even a few Tony Bennett songs. As the babies would start to calm down, I would say to myself, "I got her." And usually, I did.

There's no right or wrong way to do this, but that's what worked for me. The combination of my words and my touch, as I held them close to my chest, seemed to help these babies settle down and sleep. Of course, the nurses would crack up at my song selections.

After a couple of months of tender, loving care, Lily was well enough to be released from the hospital. I suppose she ended up in foster care.

If there were ever a kid I would have loved to take home, it would have been Lily.

A newborn baby was brought to our ED after a cleaning crew discovered him in a bag they thought contained trash. The crew was cleaning an office building when they heard a small cry emanating from the bag. The newborn was covered in blood and afterbirth, his umbilical cord still attached.

"Baby Boy," as he was named temporarily, was admitted into the PICU where I would hold him later that day. Local television stations were widely reporting the story, and our hospital was dealing with dozens of calls from people who wanted to adopt this baby.

His nurses told me they were having trouble getting him to take

My New Purpose

a bottle and asked me to try. I placed the nipple on his lips and gently turned it, and he took it in his mouth. Just after a couple of small gulps he stopped, so I turned it again, and he took a little more. He drank hardly anything, but we were encouraged that his instinct to suck was beginning to develop.

On my next shift two days later, I learned Baby Boy had been transferred to another part of the hospital. I didn't look for him because, by now, there was another baby in his old crib, one who needed me more.

My New Purpose

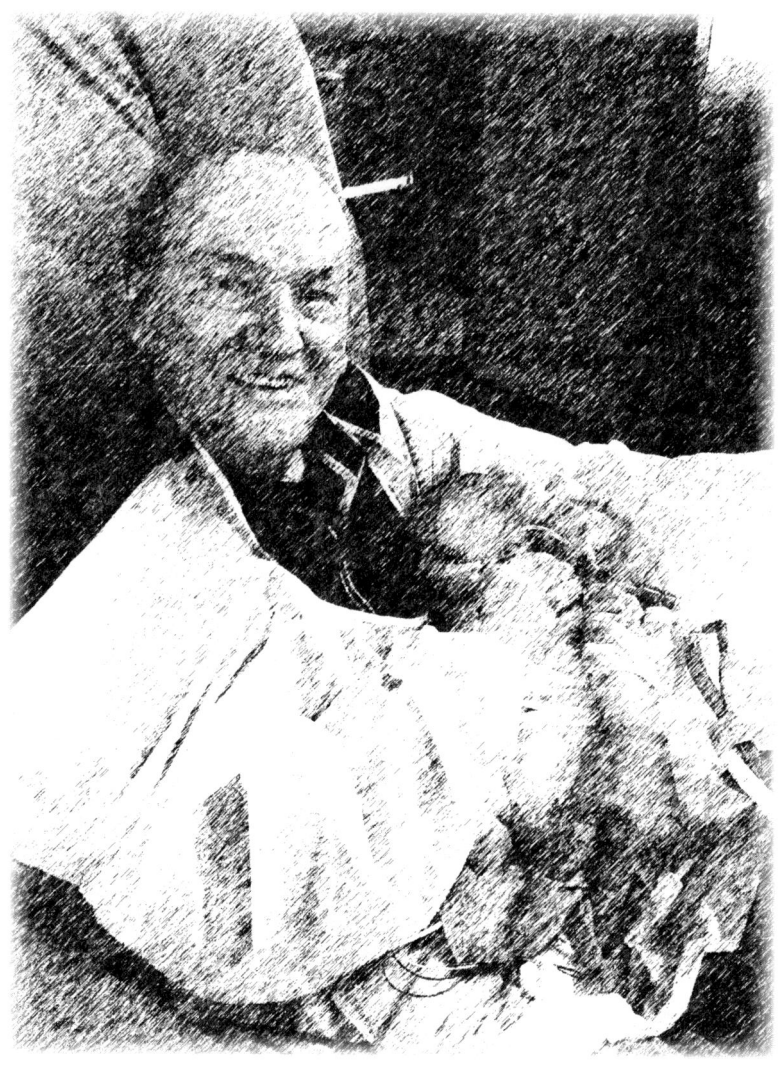

David comforts one of the hundreds of babies he's held over the years in the Children's Hospital ICU.

[34]

The Xbox Factor

THERE WAS A BAD CAR ACCIDENT during my first couple of days back in the PICU. A father and his 11-year-old son were traveling on a multilane highway when a vehicle travelling in the wrong direction hit them head-on. The father was pronounced dead on the scene and his son, Paul, was flown to Children's in critical condition.

After a few months, Paul's condition was improving but he wouldn't speak and seemed very distant. Technically speaking, he had what's called "altered mental status," or what staff sometimes referred to as "amsy."

Eventually, Paul went to the PCA since he no longer required intensive care. I often found him sitting in his room with his mom, but he still wasn't communicating, not even a smile. But then I had an idea.

I decided to get the Xbox from the PICU and see if he wanted to play. I figured before his accident, he probably played games like this. Maybe it would be the spark that helped get him to be more verbal.

The moment I rolled the Xbox stand into his room, Paul locked eyes on it and produced a giant smile, one that was immediately noticed by his mother. I plugged in the game and explained that he was going to be in charge of figuring out how to play. Well, that wasn't a problem: He completely took over.

By the next day, Paul was talking, so I asked his nurses to keep that Xbox in his room. Paul continued to make good progress and was discharged a few weeks later.

Sometimes we had a patient who was doing well and I could interface with him, kid around a little, and have some fun. I was visiting a five-year-old girl in the PICU, and she was an engaging child. There was a wastepaper can in front of her bed to the left side. I took a few paper towels, wet them, and rolled them into balls. Now we could play basketball, so I made a toss, right into the basket, and wildly congratulated myself. She, of course, said, "Can I have a turn?"

I put rubber gloves on her hands and gave her a "ball." She missed the first two times and then sank a three-pointer. The two of us went crazy celebrating, yelling "score" and giving each other high fives.

After a few more minutes, I told her I had other kids I needed to visit. She understood but had one condition. She said, "That's okay, but if you need to go, you have to do a tap dance as you leave. And after you're outside the room, you need to keep tap dancing so the nurses can see you." Then she added, "And I'm going to be watching you."

So I did a tap dance out of her room and then continued in the hallway. She was totally laughing hysterically. I don't think she believed I would actually do it.

Then I was asked to help out in the ED. I met a 12-year-old boy from New York City who came into the ED with a laceration on his hand, nothing serious. I started talking to him about New York, and I told him that I grew up in the Bronx.

After a while of kidding around with him, I told him that even though I loved New York, I couldn't understand why they didn't have a football team anymore. Of course, he claimed the Giants and the Jets were the New York football teams. I told him they didn't count because, after all, they played in New Jersey.

My New Purpose

I could see he was about to go crazy so, of course, I kept going. I asked him, "If the Chicago Bears moved to Memphis, would they still be the Chicago Bears, or would they be the Memphis Bears?" When I felt I had tortured him enough, I laughed and gave him a pat on his back.

I saw him later in the examining room and asked how his hand was doing. He said he needed four stitches and all was good. Then I leaned closer to him and said, "Are you sure they didn't say 104? Because that you might notice." He was hysterical.

[35]

The Dads

I HAVE WRITTEN MOSTLY about the children and their parents, usually just the moms I came to know at Children's Hospital. But sometimes a few of the dads stood out because of how they dealt—or didn't—with their child's situation.

I have seen several children discharged with compromised conditions or special needs that would clearly require a lifetime of care. This was a challenging situation for any family, but when Dad abandoned them because of the stress of it all, Mom was often left to raise the child alone.

I hadn't seen that happen very often, but it occurred frequently enough that I noticed it. When I did, I gave that mom a special hug, though inside I knew she needed and deserved so much more.

Sometimes dads "checked out" in an entirely different way.

I had spent a lot of time with a baby who had abdominal surgery that left him with a colostomy bag. On this particular morning, I had held him for three hours as he awaited surgery to have the bag removed and be "hooked up" again. He hadn't been allowed to eat since the night before and was in a great deal of distress.

During that time, his teenage father walked in and sat down next to me. I asked him if he would like to hold his baby before he went to surgery. He replied, "Nah, I don't like to get too close to that shit bag." I guessed that he wouldn't be volunteering to change many diapers.

But then there were the dads who became very involved with their child's care. With newborns in the NICU or sick or injured children in the PICU, there were many dads who visited as often as their circumstances would allow. And there were times when Dad would display the same emotions as Mom, including the tears, the screaming, and—on occasion—going down to the floor in their grief.

Then there were the dads who were always there, including a few that surprised me: Dads who were in the military.

I'd met three different dads over the years who were on active duty in the Army when their children were patients in the ICU. In each case, they were able to spend a great deal of time at the hospital with their child, much more time than I ever thought the military would allow.

One dad had a baby who was born with a defect that would almost certainly become fatal before his second birthday. Mom was there every day, and even though Dad was stationed about one hundred miles away, he was there nearly all of the time.

Another father had a son who was terminally ill for several months. Dad was always there with him, right up to the end.

In the third case, there were two sons critically injured in a motor vehicle accident. One died in the PICU within 48 hours, and the younger one remained in the PICU for several months, ultimately being transferred to a hospital closer to Dad's base, about 600 miles away. Once again, Dad was always there.

I am grateful to our military for giving these soldiers as much time as they needed to be with their families, and I know they are, too.

[36]

Final Thoughts

WHEN I STARTED TO WRITE about my experiences at Children's Hospital, I had no idea where I wanted it to go and how it would evolve. And now, over a year later, I have found that it's taken me to some places I never thought I would write about.

It was interesting to me that while I went through all of these experiences, I never lost my composure or broke down—in the hospital, that is.

I did find on a few occasions that, while reading a book at home, I would catch myself staring at the same page for 20 minutes, suspended in thought about the kids and, in most cases, the last child with whom I was involved. Sometimes I wouldn't even be aware of my prolonged distraction until I would suddenly feel tears running down my face.

One of my favorite authors once wrote that "95% of what happens in our lives is the result of two or three decisions." I had no way of knowing that one of those decisions—volunteering at Children's Hospital—would yield 12 years of such meaningful experiences and memories.

Towards the end of each year, the hospital has two memorial services to honor the children who have died during the past year

My New Purpose

or in years before. The larger service is for any child who has passed from any other unit of the hospital. The smaller service is just for the babies we lost in the NICU. I typically attend this service and I usually know most, if not all, of the babies who have died and their parents. In one service, I was asked to get up and say a few words, which I was honored to do.

Both services include prayers, lighting a candle for each child who was lost, and sharing hugs with other parents, the chaplains, nurses, and doctors.

Events like these remind us that not all of the children get better, which is why it's so important to celebrate those who did and memorialize those who did not.

But the darkest times for me are when I allow myself to think of what these parents who lost their child must endure. I cannot imagine all of the painful reminders at various stages of the rest of their lives. "Next month will be our first Christmas dinner without him" and "This is the week she would have been starting kindergarten."

Writing this book has forced me to process some of my most indelible memories from my experiences at Children's Hospital. The hundreds of children I've met, come to adore, and delighted in their being discharged, returning home healthier and happier, are clearly among the best of memories. Then there are the children who left the hospital with disabilities and life-long special needs, or those who never went home at all.

They will always be in my heart, all of them.

Finally, I will never forget the amazingly strong parents, fighting alongside their children, and how honored I felt to sit beside them during their most delicate and vulnerable periods of joy, tears, and—at times—incredible heartbreak.

My New Purpose

As devastating as these experiences and memories have been—some of the most intense of my life—I still wouldn't trade the last 12 years for anything. Even after writing this book, it still seems impossible to fully express how much The Kids at Children's Hospital have touched my heart and enriched my life.

My New Purpose

David celebrating his 70th birthday with daughter, Susan; wife, Ronnie; and daughter, Jill.

David and his wife, Ronnie, in Telluride, Colorado, 2004.

My New Purpose

David pictured with his daughter, Susan, and son-in-law, Jim, after one of the dozens of road races he completed during his more than 30 years as a runner.

David's grandchildren, Eli and Ryan.

My New Purpose

David and his daughter, Susan, working on his book.

David taking a break from writing.

David and Ronnie celebrate the completion of his book.

Appendix

Abbreviations

ICU: Intensive Care Unit
PICU: Pediatric Intensive Care Unit
NICU: Neonatal Intensive Care Unit
TICU: Technology-Dependent Intensive Care Unit
ER/ED: Emergency Room, now called the Emergency Department
PCA: Patient Care Areas
PA: Physician Assistant
NP: Nurse Practitioner
RT: Respiratory Therapist
PT: Physical Therapist
OT: Occupational Therapist
OR: Operating Room

BORN AND RAISED in the Bronx, New York, David Deutchman served in the U.S. Army in the early fifties during the Korean War, which included an assignment with the Presidential Honor Guard. After leaving the Army, he began a 41-year business career with Maidenform Worldwide, Inc., first as a salesman and, ultimately, as Senior Vice President for International Sales.

David married in 1962, and he and his wife, Ronnie, have two adult children, Susan and Jill, and two grandchildren, Eli and Ryan.

After retirement, David sought out volunteer work that would bring newfound meaning into his life, and he discovered it at a children's hospital.

Over the last 12 years, David has held and comforted hundreds of babies, children, and many of their parents. Now, at age 83, he sees no reason to quit.